Living Up to Your School Mission Statement

Living Up to Your School Mission Statement

Reforming Schools from the Inside Out

Alan C. Jones

ROWMAN & LITTLEFIELD
Lanham • Boulder • New York • London

Published by Rowman & Littlefield
An imprint of The Rowman & Littlefield Publishing Group, Inc.
4501 Forbes Boulevard, Suite 200, Lanham, Maryland 20706
www.rowman.com

6 Tinworth Street, London, SE11 5AL, United Kingdom

Copyright © 2021 by Alan C. Jones

All rights reserved. No part of this book may be reproduced in any form or by any electronic or mechanical means, including information storage and retrieval systems, without written permission from the publisher, except by a reviewer who may quote passages in a review.

British Library Cataloguing in Publication Information Available

Library of Congress Cataloging-in-Publication Data

Names: Jones, Alan C. (associate professor), author.
Title: Living up to your school mission statement : reforming schools from the inside out / Alan C. Jones.
Description: Lanham : Rowman & Littlefield, [2021] | Includes bibliographical references. | Summary: "This books summarizes the political, cultural, and institutional drivers of the disconnect between what administrators say from auditorium stages and what they do in their offices"—Provided by publisher.
Identifiers: LCCN 2021026581 (print) | LCCN 2021026582 (ebook) | ISBN 9781475862911 (cloth) | ISBN 9781475862928 (paperback) | ISBN 9781475862935 (epub)
Subjects: LCSH: Education—Aims and objectives. | School management and organization. | Educational planning. | Educational leadership. | Mission statements.
Classification: LCC LA210 .J57 2021 (print) | LCC LA210 (ebook) | DDC 370.11—dc23
LC record available at https://lccn.loc.gov/2021026581
LC ebook record available at https://lccn.loc.gov/2021026582

For

Tyler, Sebastian, and Deacon

May the classrooms they sit in live up to their school's mission statement

Contents

Acknowledgments	xi
Introduction	1
District 93's Mission Statement	1
Independence School District Mission Statement	1
District 85's Set of Beliefs	2
When Mission Meets Reality	2
Theoretical Drivers	3
Managerial Drivers	4
Governmental Drivers	6
Community Drivers	6
Institutional Drivers	7
Reforming Schools from the Inside Out	8
The Structure of this Book	9
Terminology	12
What is a REFORM INITIATIVE?	12
What is INSTITUTIONAL SCHOOLING?	13
What is a MINDSET?	13
What is an ECLECTIC LEADER?	16
What are GOALS AND VALUES?	16
1 The Goal Maze	21
Goal Triage	22
Absentee Landlords	25
Technocrats	25
Bureaucrats	26
True Believers	26
The Proper Vetting of School Goals	27

	Standing Goal Triage on its Head	28
	Why Am I Here?	29
	RESOURCES	31
2	Championing	39
	What Kind of Organization Am I Leading?	40
	Managing, Leading, and Championing	40
	Championing a Mathematical Vision	43
	Becoming a Strong Champion	45
	Working in the Margins of School Organizations	50
	RESOURCES	52
3	Main Office C	59
	The Forms of Schooling	59
	The Functions of Education	61
	Main Office A and B	63
	Getting to Main Office C	65
	The Dilemma of Main Office C	65
	RESOURCES	68
4	Silver Bullets	71
	Telling, Selling, Installing	72
	Assessing and Facilitating	74
	Pulling the Trigger	77
	RESOURCES	78
5	Following Through	81
	Following Up	82
	Following Through	83
	The Decision to Follow Through	84
	Following Up or Following Through on Common Core	86
	Following Through on School Mission Statements	90
	RESOURCES	92
6	The Crisis of the Day	95
	Fixing Problems: The Blame Game	95
	Fixing the Crisis of the Day	97
	Solving the Crisis of the Day: Food Fights in the Cafeteria	99
	Doing the Right Thing	102
	The Entrepreneur	103
	RESOURCES	107
7	Noticing	109
	The Noise and the Signs of Schooling	109
	Noticing Values	111

8	Tools in the Toolbox	113
	The Cycle of Reform Failure	114
	Putting the Tools Together	116
	RESOURCES	118
9	Getting to YES	121
	Institutional NOs	121
	Getting to YES	123
	Creating Value in Your School Organization	127
10	Restoring the Why to Schooling	129
	The Dilemma of Institutional Schooling	130
	Eclectic Leaders	132
References		135
About the Author		137

Acknowledgments

The idea for this book originated from a conversation I had with a colleague of my mine, whose consulting firm specialized in writing school district strategic plans. While describing his work, he said to me: "The worse part of the job is writing the school's mission statement. It really slows down the whole exercise. You know how that goes; you spend hours posting feel-good goals on conference walls that you know will never see the light of day in classrooms." "He went on to say that at least the exercise served to "break the ice" for writing an action plan.

The frustration expressed by my colleague represents a managerial mindset focused on the *what* and *how* of running a school well. While no school administrator would doubt the importance of a well-run school, the *why* of schooling is lost in this singular pursuit of managerial goals. Without a foundational purpose of schooling—the *why*—the inspirational goals of schooling are cast aside when the focus is only on complying with governmental mandates and executing managerial functions—reforming schooling from the outside in.

This book offers school administrators a framework for refocusing the occupants of central and district offices on the *why* of schooling. The refocusing of managerial mindsets on what really matters in schools—*why are we here?*—provides a platform for redefining what teachers do in classrooms and how they do it—transforming schools from the inside out.

My own experience with transforming the *ought* of educational ideals into the *is* of classroom practice—reforming school from the inside out—was guided by three mentors whose differing perspectives on mission-driven goals formulated in my mind the ties between the *why*, *what*, and *how*, of enacting mission-driven practices in classrooms. Maury Gladstone taught me that mission-driven goals do matter in schools. George Bieber taught me that behind every mission-driven goal is a well-designed system. Richard Kamm taught me that no matter how worthwhile a mission-driven goal maybe, politics will have the last say.

Along with these lessons, I was fortunate to work with like-minded colleagues who joined with me in assimilating mission-driven goals into the classrooms and offices they supervised. Among those educators with whom I worked to reform a school from the inside out were Marjorie Appel, Tom Arnold, Gail Aronoff, Maura Bridges, Joe Crickard, John Highland, Beth Hunter, Paul Junkroski, Tom McCann, Marianne Melvin, George Strecker, Dick Waterhouse, and Lee Yunker.

My ongoing quest to articulate the lessons learned in working with schools from the inside out can be largely attributed to a continuing conversation with my outside assistant, Amy Daly. Amy's comments in the margins always brought clarity to my writing, but, more importantly, helped me to question the assumptions I make about my audience.

Introduction

Vision without action is merely a dream.
Action without vision just passes time.
Vision with action can change the world.
(Joel Barker)

DISTRICT 93'S MISSION STATEMENT

District 93 seeks to create a challenging learning environment that encourages high expectations for success through developmentally appropriate instruction that allows for individual differences and learning styles. Our school establishes values to act with thoughtfulness and a sense of understanding and compassion for others. Each student's self-esteem is fostered by positive relationships with students and staff. We strive to have our parents, teachers, and community members actively involved in our students' learning.

INDEPENDENCE SCHOOL DISTRICT MISSION STATEMENT

The challenge for schools today is to meet the needs of students for tomorrow—to ready our youth for living and working in a globalized world very different from both the present and the past. We believe that education is vital for developing the social, emotional, and intellectual skills of young children and adolescents. Our mission at Independence School District is to further develop the intellectual, vocational, creative, aesthetic, and physical capabilities of our diverse student body. Our commitment is to provide intellectually engaging learning environments; to develop the knowledge, skills, and dispositions needed for an ever-changing world beyond high school; and to nurture the individual interests, talents, and abilities of our student body. We believe that quality staff is key to providing quality education. We are dedicated to the development of professional and personal knowledge and skills of our staff members. We encourage the cooperation and involvement of parents and other community members in our educational process.

DISTRICT 85'S SET OF BELIEFS

- An effective school climate promotes mutual respect, open communication, shared decision-making, and individuality.
- Quality education requires a collaborative effort.
- A community and its resources are important to a child's education.
- Risk-taking and change are valuable and essential to growth.
- Cognitive, social, emotional, physical, and aesthetic growth are of equal importance.
- Understanding cultural similarities and differences is essential to growth and development.
- Students have an active and responsible role in making decisions affecting their school experience.
- A meaningful curriculum fosters problem-solving, high-level thinking skills, and reflects on real life.
- All children should have equal access to high-quality learning experiences.
- Learning best occurs in a safe environment that provides appropriate limits and promotes respect for self and others.

WHEN MISSION MEETS REALITY

All school districts have written statements of the educational values and goals that members of the school community believe are important and worth pursuing. They display these on the front page of all school district public relations packets and on the walls of school and district offices. While all segments of the school community enthusiastically embrace the values and goals stated in the documents, rarely, if ever, do they practice these goals and values in classrooms or administrative offices.

The gap between the educational ideals spoken from auditorium stages and the instructional regimes students experience in classrooms is the result of schools designed to achieve institutional goals—accountability, standardization, and efficiency—rather than educational goals—thoughtfulness, deep knowledge, and critically informed citizens. The structure and direction of our school systems are unsurprising when one considers the institutional methods of public schooling: compulsory attendance and credentialing. These approaches create organizational structures that prize order over disruption, routinization over novelty, and accountability over responsibility.

For the most part, the obvious gap between the goals and values expressed in school mission statements and the classroom realities experienced by students goes unnoticed by members of the school community. After opening-day references to critical thinking, lifelong learning, and caring learning communities, administrators return to their offices to *manage* bureaucratic routines, teachers return to their classrooms to *manage* instructional routines, and students return to rows of desk to *manage* the daily classroom routines of listening, completing worksheets, and taking tests.

As the days and months of the school year wear on, some members of the school community will recognize, even voice frustration over, the gaps between the aims of schooling expressed in school mission statements and the functions of schooling practiced in administrative offices and classrooms. None of these outbreaks of frustration reference specific terminology from school mission statements. Mission statement vocabularies do not translate well into school and classroom functions designed to move large numbers of students through a school day and through a course of study. In fact, the terminology that accurately describes factory-style schooling is in direct opposition to the goals and values expressed in school mission statements: critical thinking becomes reciting facts and procedures; collaborative learning communities become assigned groups working on contrived schooling problems; well-prepared for college and career pathways becomes class ranking and number of advanced courses completed; and one student at a time becomes pull-out remedial programs.

Why is this obvious disconnect between educational ideals and organizational realities overlooked by most school communities? What follows is a summary of political, cultural, and institutional drivers of the disconnect between what administrators say from auditorium stages and what they do in their offices.

THEORETICAL DRIVERS

Implementing the "How"

School communities purposefully design mission statements to make everyone feel good about the taxes they pay, the schools they send their students to, and the offices and classrooms in which they work. To achieve the desired level of enthusiasm and commitment to schooling, mission statements utilize terminology that is both emotionally appealing and open to wide interpretation. What member of a strategic planning committee would not feel a source of pride knowing they are preparing young people to *excel in a complex, interconnected, changing world* or to *flourish as a responsible citizen in the global community* or to become *lifelong learners with the knowledge, skills, and values required for productive global citizenship*? Nowhere in these strategic planning sessions, however, is any time allocated for *how* to implement these educational abstractions in classrooms.

Knowledge of the "How"

Even if the *how* is discussed at strategic planning sessions, few educators in the room have the necessary historical, philosophical, or instructional backgrounds to properly educate the school community on alternative ways of thinking about and practicing schooling. School communities reward administrators for efficiently managing the organizational and instructional routines already in place. They do not reward those who disrupt the daily grammar of institutional schooling or attempt to reeducate the school community on how to achieve the educational goals and values listed in school mission statements.

MANAGERIAL DRIVERS

Losing Control

The greatest fear of any sitting school administrator is losing control over the forms of schooling and the functions of teaching. Administrators view any form of dysfunctionality—absenteeism, gangs, fights, or drugs—as a threat to their livelihoods. Early on in their careers, school administrators learn how to manage institutional tools designed to control the behaviors and movement of student populations: schedules, rules, penalties, and labels. Administrators utilize these institutional tools believing that fear and custom will induce a compliance mentality that results in what Sarason (1997) termed the "regularities" of schooling. Twenty-five-minute lunches, fifty-minute periods, late bells, grades, credits, and suspensions are among the favored institutional tools that guarantee every school day will be uneventful.

The organizational and pedagogical uncertainties built into progressive instructional regimes are a bridge too far for most main offices. School administrators are much more comfortable managing seven-period days and seven-step lesson plans than supervising open classrooms and project-based learning.

Budget, Boilers, and Boosters

There are two distinct career trajectories presented to aspiring school administrators: the managerial trajectory of budgets, boilers, and boosters; or the instructional trajectory of curriculum and instruction. The trajectory that an administrator chooses determines the level and speed of advancement. School administrators who fill their resumes with managerial accomplishments—completing building projects, balancing budgets, and successfully mediating special interest grievances—quickly rise to upper-tier positions in school administration—principals, assistant superintendents, and superintendents. School administrators who fill their resumes with instructional accomplishments—writing curriculum, designing staff development programs, and implementing teacher evaluation plans—remain in lower-tier positions in school administration—assistant principals, administrative assistants, department chairs, and directors.

Although school administrators and board of education members publicly proclaim their devotion to the role of instructional leader, in private they honor the role of CEO—the managerial trajectory. With this private understanding in place, career-minded administrators position themselves for administrative assignments demonstrating that they are made of the right managerial stuff. The knowledge and skills required to live up to the educational goals in school mission statements atrophy over time, and eventually, all but disappear in calendars crowded with budget meetings, strategic planning sessions, Lions Club luncheons, and county board meetings.

Managerial Mindsets

When school board members and administrators leave a strategic planning retreat, both groups feel very good about their role in authoring a vision of schooling committed to achieving the educational goals and values listed on break-out room wall charts. Both groups, however, leave these break-out rooms with different understandings of what these goals and values will look like inside classrooms. School board members and administrators translate vision statements into questions of *implementation*: *When* will the goal be implemented? *How much* will the new goal cost to implement? The answers to these questions call for simple managerial responses: announced timelines, projected budgets, purchased materials, personnel hires, and documentation of managerial goals.

The questions that are never asked in main office conference rooms are the instructional questions associated with teaching the educational goal or values: *What* is the instructional meaning of the goal? *How* will that goal look in classrooms? *How* will teachers teach that goal? School board members and administrators bypass the answers to the second set of questions with the managerial belief that competent performance of managerial functions will be translated into the competent performance of educational functions.

GOVERNMENTAL DRIVERS

Mandates

The educational goals listed in school mission statements are not the same goals valued by governmental bodies. Main office in-boxes are filled with forms and memoranda directing school administrators to implement a long list of mandated institutional goals: maintaining accurate records of daily attendance; documenting the completion of prescribed course requirements; certifying the reliable administration of state testing programs; implementing the mandate of the year (No Child Left Behind, Race to the Top, Common Core Standards); verifying teacher certification requirements; and complying with governing boards' policies and procedures. As long as the procedures of the mandate are complied with, administrators assume the substance of the mandate will take care of itself.

Race to the Top

The last two decades of school reform policies have been dominated by managerial tools designed to measure and judge a school's performance. All of these accountability instruments, from standardized tests to value-added teacher evaluations, are simply more tools in managerial toolboxes. Each of these tools, however, is unable to measure any of the *educational* goals and values written into school mission statements—critical thinking, lifelong learning, productive global citizenship, and preparation to excel in a complex, interconnected, and changing world. They measure fragments of subject matter knowledge very well—facts and procedures. While these fragments of knowledge are necessary for supporting the educational outcomes listed in school mission statements, they are not sufficient for certifying a student's ability to orchestrate these fragments of knowledge and skills into political, economic, and social strategies that solve real-world problems.

COMMUNITY DRIVERS

Forms of Schooling

A superintendent said to me after a particularly hostile community response to a proposed innovative interdisciplinary program, "Well, Al, the problem with school reform is everyone has been to third grade." What he meant by that comment is that all parents have been well-schooled in the *forms* of schooling: periods, subjects, grades, tests, homework, ranking, notes, and review sheets. Most parents have never experienced the substance of schooling—the goals and values listed in school mission statements. School communities will oppose any new program that modifies or eliminates something they know a lot about—a form of schooling—in exchange for something they know little or nothing about—the substance of schooling.

INSTITUTIONAL DRIVERS

Organizational Infrastructure

The entire professional infrastructure of public schooling in this country is grounded in the beliefs, values, and practices of a bureaucratic model of schooling that values simplicity over complexity, standardization over novelty, and stability over disruption. The chief tasks of a school administrator working in a bureaucratic model of schooling are to *define what is real* (mandates, data, credentials, and credits); *to reduce uncertainties* (using rules, regulations, procedures, and schedules); and *to increase performance* (with standards, measures, and feedback). None of these managerial tools, materials, systems, or organizational structures is designed to address the social, emotional, and intellectual themes listed in school mission statements: *"critical thinking," "lifelong learning," "engaged learner," and "develop individual talents and abilities."*

Thanks for Your Comment

The last item on main office meeting agendas is a section labeled, *"Comments."* Newly hired administrators, sitting at the end of conference tables, view this agenda item as an opportunity to share a new idea or practice they believe will help the school live up to its mission statement. Experienced administrators sitting at the head of conference tables, view this agenda item as a perfunctory display of a collaborative team environment. Any hope of using this agenda item to question established organizational or instructional routines is quickly dashed when the chair of the meeting issues the final edict on the *comment* section of the meeting agenda: *"Thanks, Tom, for your input. Our next meeting date is _____."* It does not take long for new administrators to learn that talk of innovative approaches to teaching and learning will earn them a permanent seat at the end of main office conference tables.

Circumstances beyond Your Control

Even when school administrators are committed to living up to their schools' mission statements, outside circumstances enter the main office and often undermine the implementation and enactment of educational goals and values. Table I.1 summarizes the political, organizational, and cultural circumstances that commonly occur during a school year. Depending on the history of the district and school, each circumstance possesses the potential to derail any initiatives designed to implement an educational goal or value listed in a school mission statement.

Districts and schools possessing strong and stable leadership, a coherent instructional worldview, strong parent-community ties, and a strong professional culture possess the capacity to neutralize the force of these destructive circumstances. Schools without these strong organizational and professional pillars in place will see the educational goals and values announced from auditorium stages ignored or marginalized.

REFORMING SCHOOLS FROM THE INSIDE OUT

Every school day, the institutional and community drivers of bureaucratic schooling come together in main offices, hallways, and classrooms to create organizational and instructional practices that routinely displace the *why* of schooling with managerial *what's* and *how's* of schooling. This book is aimed at school administrators whose personal and professional goal is to reverse the priorities of schooling in America—restoring the *why* of schooling to the organizational structures and instructional routines that currently govern public schooling in this nation.

Table I.1   Circumstances beyond Your Control

SOURCE	CIRCUMSTANCES
Political	• Changing membership of the board of education • Turnover in Superintendent's office • Governmental mandates • Community concerns
Organizational	• Inadequate resources • Inadequate technology • Inadequate space • Inadequate systems
Personnel	• Teacher turnover • Administrative turnover • Illness/Death
Cultural	• Strong belief systems can lead to resistance • Weak belief systems can lead to disorder

A substantial amount of school reform literature exists that addresses the misplaced priorities of public schooling—what Thomas J. Sergiovanni (1992), has termed the repurposing of our schools. Much of this literature calls for school leaders to install programs or acquire lists of leadership qualities to modify or purge schools of the bureaucratic drivers of public schooling—reforming schools from the *outside in*.

Reforming schools from the *outside in* ignores a model of schooling which, for the most part, school communities believe, not only works, but works very well. The graveyard of school reform initiatives is filled with mandates, programs, and leadership strategies designed to replace a form of schooling with the substance of schooling.

The drivers of institutional schooling are here to stay: *school boards* will continue to believe their schools are pursuing the educational goals and values authored at strategic planning sessions; *school administrators* will continue to employ managerial means over educational ends; *governmental bodies* will continue to demand administrative accountability over educational responsibility; *school communities* will continue to support the forms of schooling they once attended; *administrative careers* will continue to follow managerial trajectories; and *school organizations* will continue to operate systems designed to regulate, standardize, and document.

The error that school reform advocates continually make is to assume that imposing transformational theories and pedagogies on school communities brings about reforms in organizational and instructional practices. The managerial and leadership strategies described in this book turn this school reform maxim on its head. Instead of searching for or implementing a mandate or program designed to *transform* a driver of institutional schooling, the occupants of main offices should concentrate on *reforming* the organizational and instructional practices that support each driver—reforming school from the *inside out*.

THE STRUCTURE OF THIS BOOK

Each chapter in this book is divided into two sections. Section one of each chapter identifies a managerial practice that blocks administrators and teachers from pursuing the educational goals and values written into school mission statements. Section two of each chapter describes a managerial and leadership strategy that school administrators could employ to redirect a school community's attention away from the *forms* of schooling and toward the *substance* of schooling—living up to a school's mission statement.

Chapter 1 describes the *Goal Maze* that school administrators find themselves trapped in each year. The maze is composed of long lists of institutional goals—mandates, policies, and programs—that lie in main office in-boxes. Each of these institutional goals forms a maze whose twists and turns are designed around goals that are unclear ("love of learning"), goals that contradict each other (standardize/individuate), and goals that are unachievable ("equality"). Walking into the middle of this maze, school administrators are assigned the responsibility for guiding teachers and students through the maze without fundamentally changing the design or the content of the maze. School administrators employ a series of managerial moves—goal triage—giving the appearance of moving *through* the maze, but in reality, only moving teachers and students around *within* the maze. School administrators intent on achieving the educational goals and practices written into school mission statements circumvent the goal maze by questioning the purposes, worth, and feasibility of each goal that enters main offices.

Chapter 2 introduces a new form of school leadership fashioned around a pattern of strategizing aimed at embedding the educational goals and values written into school mission statements within the structures of institutional schooling. Main offices are heavily populated with managerial mindsets that abhor the ambiguities and uncertainties brought on by the pursuit of the educational goals and values written into school mission statements. *Champions* overcome these managerial fears by weaving together the functions of manager, leader, and champion into an administrative stance that achieves educational ends without disturbing organizational means—reforming schools from the inside out.

Chapter 3 examines the three forms of main offices school administrators walk into each day: Main office A, B, and C. Main Office A is filled with bureaucratic structures organized to tell, allocate, and inspect. Main Office B has professional structures organized to train, classify, and assess. Main Office C contains an educational structure organized to educate, facilitate, and coach. Administrators in Main Office C enter their offices each day with the goal of aligning the *aims of schooling*—goals and values listed in school mission statements—with the *functions of schooling*—what administrators and teachers actually perform in their respective workspaces. Institutional forms of schooling that are in direct opposition to the goals and values written into school mission statements stand between aims and functions of schooling. Administrators in Main Office C make collective sense out of offices organized around contradictory goals and methods. To successfully adopt pedagogies that live up to the goals and values of school mission statements, administrators in Main Office C carry out the functions of learning a new model of teaching without disturbing the forms of schooling.

Chapters 4 and 5 look at two organizational tools that managerial mindsets employ to project an image of living up to a school's mission statement. Chapter 4 describes how managerial mindsets use *Silver Bullet Programs* to prove their commitment to the educational goals and values written into their school mission statements. Silver Bullet programs are so attractive to managerial mindsets because the certainties of administrating the artifacts of the program—distributing materials, scheduling in-service workshops, or administering assessment instruments—don't require mastering the subjective understandings of the theories and practices governing the program. Without paying full attention to understanding the theories and practices of Silver Bullet programs, the educational value of these programs is never fully realized.

Chapter 5 describes the role that the feedback function—"touching base"—plays in maintaining the organizational and instructional routines of institutional schooling. Managers narrowly define feedback as *following up* on the completion of institutional tasks: materials accounted for, timelines met, data collected, budgets met, and accountability forms turned in. Educational mindsets expand the definition of the feedback function to include *following through* on processes designed to make collective sense out of concepts, theories, and practices in a new program initiative.

Chapter 6 examines how managerial and educational mindsets think about and act upon schoolwide problems that do not respond to managerial fixes—*the crisis of the day*. Managerial mindsets react to disruptions to well-rehearsed organizational and instructional routines with a managerial *fix*: add a resource, employ additional personnel, redesign a system, or write a new policy. When these managerial fixes fail to solve the disruption, school administrators blame outside forces beyond their control—students, parents, or society—for their failure to restore certainty to their school organization. Educational mindsets *solve* the crisis of the day by inviting members of the school community into a messy inquiry process that consists of part theory, part prediction, part practice, and part experimentation. The goal of adding value to the school organization—living up to the school's mission statement—holds this messy process together.

Chapter 7 looks at the symbolic role *noticing* plays in living up to the educational values and practices written into school mission statements. Schools are designed to notice disruptions to the goals and practices of institutional schooling. A late bus, a bell that does not ring, grades not handed in, graffiti in washrooms, and large groups of students standing in hallways are disruptions that draw the notice of managerial mindsets. School administrators are judged on how adept they are at silencing the noise of schooling. S*igns* that the educational values written into school mission statements are not being lived up to go unnoticed when silencing the *noise* of schooling. Is a student standing outside of a classroom during a period of the *noise* of adolescent misbehavior, or is it a *sign* that learners are not being engaged in meaningful learning experiences? Is an accident report the *noise* of adolescent carelessness, or a *sign* of an unsafe learning environment?

Chapter 8 describes the contrast between managerial and educational tools lying in main office toolboxes. Managerial mindsets reach for those tools designed to implement the products of a new instructional initiative. Educational mindsets reach for those tools designed to make collective sense out of theories, ideas, and practices. Both sets of tools are necessary for implementing successful educational initiatives. Without the educational tools—teaching, facilitating, and coaching—administrators and teachers lack processes to make collective sense out of new instructional theories and practices. Without the organizational tools—telling, allocating, and inspecting—administrators lack the processes to incorporate new instructional theories and instructional practices into established institutional structures.

Chapter 9 describes the managerial thinking behind the customary managerial response to efforts to live up to the educational goals and values in the school mission statement: *the institutional NO*. Teachers rarely become upset with this institutional response. They have come to expect that requests for more flexibility, more time, more space, or more expertise, will be met with three institutional responses: we have no choice, we cannot change, or we do not have the resources. Mission-driven administrators find ways of getting around *the institutional no* and getting to *the educational YES*. The chapter presents cases describing how school administrators created spaces within *the institutional no* for an *educational yes*.

The final chapter in this book describes a new leadership construct that allows school administrators to create and actualize the right balance between managerial means and educational ends. Caught in the tug-of-war between the managerial realities of main offices and the educational ideals written into school mission statements, *eclectic leaders* orchestrate the right mix of managing functions (implementation), leading functions (education), and championing functions (inventing), to make collective sense out of conflicting goals, values, and practices. All three leadership qualities weave together the why, what, and how of schooling into a narrative and plans of action that place the *ought* of schooling before the *is* of schooling.

TERMINOLOGY

WHAT IS A REFORM INITIATIVE?

Throughout this book, I use an assortment of educational and organizational terms to describe school reform initiatives specifically aimed at living up to the educational goals and values written into school mission statements: "instructional initiative," "reform initiative," "new pedagogy," and "instructional model." Although all of these terms could be interpreted as gradual changes to organizational and teaching routines, I use these terms "interchangeability" to represent teaching models based on responsive instruction: models that ask students to construct their own personal understandings of knowledge, rather replicate what teachers tell them (see table I.2). School administrators living up to their schools' mission statements create spaces in their schools to practice the kinds of teaching best suited to achieve the educational mission of schooling.

WHAT IS INSTITUTIONAL SCHOOLING?

Our society is built upon the backs of institutions. Every activity we engage in has been formed by the roles, rules, and routines of the institutions with which we come in contact. The organizational structures in school institutions shape how large groups of children and adolescents are educated. The routines of institutional schooling—seven-period days, fifty-five-minute periods, subjects, grade levels, and tests—are all designed to control, monitor, and document the behavior of student bodies. At the same time, however, these regulative structures constrain instructional models that are designed to develop the educational mission of schooling: growing the interests and talents of diverse student bodies. All main offices struggle to organize the regulative functions of schooling to achieve the educational aims of school mission statements. Mission-driven main offices reconfigure the regulative functions of institutions to service the educational aims of teaching and learning.

WHAT IS A MINDSET?

Each chapter in this book examines the mindsets that presently guide decision-making in district and school offices. A mindset is a pattern of ideas, beliefs, practices, and vocabularies that come together each day in main offices to facilitate certain kinds of actions and not others. School administrators guided by managerial mindsets (see table I.3) believe the purpose of schooling is to classify, standardize, and document teaching and learning. Managerial mindsets rely on rules, regulations, procedures, and systems to create school environments that are efficient, predictable, and accountable.

School administrators guided by educational mindsets believe the purpose of schooling is to live up to the educational goals and values written into school mission statements: to develop the diverse interests, talents, and abilities of their student bodies. Educational mindsets rely on models of teaching and school configurations designed to engage students in the levels of thinking and methods of inquiry listed in school mission statements.

School administrators guided by entrepreneurial mindsets believe the purpose of schooling is to enact out-of-the box solutions for in-box troubles: absenteeism, tardiness, low test scores, gangs, drugs, or poor community support. Entrepreneurial mindsets rely on novel ideas and practices to drive the redesign of established organizational and instructional routines so that schools are what they *ought* to be.

Table I.2 Two Traditions of Teaching

Fundamental Question of Schooling	Direct Instruction	Responsive Instruction
How do children learn?	• Imitate • Practice	• Discover • Construct
What knowledge is of greatest worth?	• Facts • Procedures • Definitions	• Big ideas • Big questions • Concepts • Theories
How should knowledge be organized?	• Textbook • Standards • Objectives • Skills	• Thematic • Interdisciplinary • Problem-based • Understandings
How should we assess what students understand?	• Summative assessments • Content aligned with objectives • Standardized tests • Evaluation • Performance	• Formative assessments • Content aligned with concepts • Authentic assessments • Feedback • Mastery
How should we teach?	• Transmission • Demonstration • Recitation • Practice • Test/grade • Rank • Individual achievement	• Listening • Inquiry (problems, cases, and scenarios) • Personal modeling • Discussion/debate • Collaboration

Adapted from: Jackson, P. W. (1986). *The Practice of Teaching*. New York: Teachers College Press.

Table I.3 Main Office Mindsets

MANAGERIAL (How and Who)	EDUCATIONAL (What and Why)	ENTREPRENURIAL (The Ought)
Systems	Mission Statements	Vision
Personnel	Programs	Theories, Ideas, Concepts
Budgets	Course Configurations	Problem-Solution Fits
Materials	Master Schedules	Experts
Time	Curriculum Handbook	Models
Space	Staff Development	Experimentation
Expertise	Professional Performance	Risk-taking

Administrators guided by these different mindsets implement goals, mandates, programs, and daily operations with different rationales and different ends in view. An administrator who expresses a belief in institutional goals and practices will spend their time in main offices telling, allocating, inspecting, and documenting. An administrator who expresses a belief in educational goals and values will spend their time in teacher workplaces educating, facilitating, coaching, and providing feedback. An administrator who expresses a discontent with institutional goals, structures, and practices, will spend their time describing the problem, mobilizing resources, enlisting quality external support, managing resistance, initiating organizational redesigns, and connecting to other schools with similar problems.

All three administrators will appear to be engaging in managerial duties and functions, but the problems they take on, where they spend their time, the vocabularies they use, the materials they purchase, how they allocate resources, how they configure systems, how they use space, how courses are configured, how teachers are evaluated, and the outcomes they expect will reflect contrasting mindsets.

Three decades of school reform have been consumed with a struggle between which mindset would govern the main offices, hallways, and classrooms of this country. Groups outside of schools—legislators, educational researchers, and consultants—have promoted a school reform agenda that favors educational and entrepreneurial mindsets over the goals, values, and practices of managerial mindsets. In their zeal to purge schools of managerial mindsets, outside school reformers miss the powerful institutional goals and practices that most school communities' value and expect those inside to maintain and uphold.

Living up to mission-driven goals is not a matter of one mindset winning over another mindset. Schools living up to their educational missions develop the capacity for all three mindsets to exist in productive tension: managerial mindsets know how to operate a school well; educational mindsets know what goals and values a school should be pursuing; and entrepreneurial mindsets see promising situations for developing novel ideas and practices. School administrators who orchestrate the right relationship between managerial means (the how and who), educational ends (the what and why), and mission statement values (what ought to be), are reforming schools from the *inside out*.

WHAT IS AN ECLECTIC LEADER?

Throughout this book, I use the generic term "school administrators" to describe those whose thinking and actions strive to live up to their schools' mission statements. I avoid labeling the thinking and functions of these same school administrators as instructional leadership. Although I have written extensively on the subject of instructional leadership (Jones 2015, 2018), I have come to realize that the leadership qualities I have described in my books are conceptual abstractions too far removed from the daily demands, constraints, and expectations that institutional schooling places on the occupants of main offices. School administrators caught between the instructional leadership "ought" of school reform literature and the managerial "is" of institutional schooling settle on an institutional version of instructional leadership—talk educationally, perform institutionally.

Living up to educational goals and values written into school mission statements need not be an either/or choice between managerial means and educational ends. Each chapter in this book describes how an Eclectic Leader goes about the task of fusing together different administrative functions—managing, leading, and championing—to bridge the gap between the institutional realities of running a school and the educational ideals they promise their school communities. Eclectic leaders are sometimes managers, sometimes leaders, and sometimes champions. At all times, eclectic leaders are committed to enacting educational functions within institutional forms of schooling.

WHAT ARE GOALS AND VALUES?

All school communities embrace the goals and values written into their school mission statements. Who in the school community would disagree with the goals of critical thinking or the value of lifelong learning? The power of mission statements is the emotional appeal of generalized beliefs about habits of thinking and personal dispositions that all parents believe their children should be taught. The weakness of mission statements is that they do not specify *how* an educational goal or value will be best taught in classrooms. The school community assumes that the managerial forms of schooling—periods, subjects, tests, and grades—will enact mission-driven goals and values. Within the profession of teaching, however, there are a variety of instructional models that teachers could employ to teach a mission-driven goal or value. Some of these instructional models teach these mission-driven goals and values better than others. Administrators intent on living up to the goals and values written into their schools' mission statements establish an educative process that asks teachers to author an agreed-upon definition of a mission-stated goal or value and to decide upon the instructional model best suited to teach that goal or value.

Each chapter in this book describes how the institutional forms of schooling serve as powerful obstacles to achieving the educational goals and values written into school mission statements. The topic of this book, however, is not an analysis of how these institutional forms of schooling marginalize educational goals and values. *Becoming a Strong Instructional Leader: Saying No to Business as Usual* (Jones 2015) and *The First 100 Days in the Main Office: Transforming a School Culture* (Jones 2018) provide that analysis by examining the source and consequences of institutional schooling.

This book is about how school administrators work around the institutional forms of schooling to achieve the educational functions of school mission statements.

In order to successfully work around the routines of institutional schooling, school administrators must have taken time to construct in their own minds an organizational and instructional framework that sees opportunities and strategies to merge the means of institutional forms with the ends of educational functions. These school administrators live up to their schools' mission statements by authoring narratives, instructional frameworks, and organizational configurations that link the why, what, and how of schooling. Figure I.1 illustrates a conceptual framework for thinking about the connection between educational goals and values and organizational and instructional routines—connecting the cultural dots. Tables I.4 through I.6 describe the meaning and organizational enactment of connecting the dots and achieving the vision.

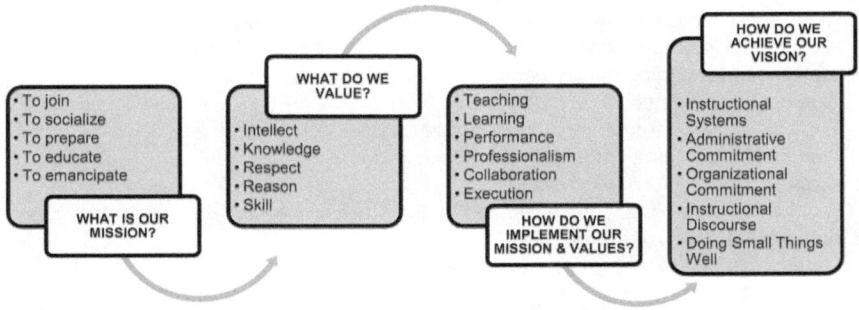

Figure I.1 Connecting the Cultural Dots.

Table I.4 Connecting the Cultural Dots—Part I

What Is Our Mission?

Join
How do I effectively participate in a democratic community?
Socialize
How should I behave?
Prepare
What do I want to become and how can I do it well?
Educate
What is true, good, and beautiful?
Emancipate
Who am I?

What Do We Value?

Intellect: *(How do we examine life?)*
True intelligence is not knowing all the answers, but knowing what questions to ask → *Teaching matters*
Knowledge: *(How do we explain life?)*
A professional knows the what, why, and how of what they are talking about → *Competence matters*
Respect: *(How do we treat each other?)*
Children learn best in environments where diverse talents, abilities, and interests are known, respected, and nurtured → *Relationships matter*
Reason: *(How do we solve problems?)*
Beliefs, judgments, and actions are supported by reasons and the evidence they provide → *Reasoning Matters*
Skill: *(How do we enact our values?)*
Successful organizations do the small things well → *Execution matters*

Table I.5 Connecting the Cultural Dots—Part II

How Do We Implement Our Mission and Values?

Teaching *(what matters most in schooling):*
Quality learning experiences are solely dependent on the employment, development, and supervision of quality teachers.
Learning *(the full engagement of a child's social need to be known, the emotional need to be interested, and the intellectual need to understand):*
All students look to schools to honor their diverse talents, abilities, and interests.
Performance *(providing quality educational experiences based on students' expectations and needs):*
The goal of all performance indicators and criteria is closing the gap between ideal models of teaching and learning and classroom realities.
Professionalism *(reflection on practice):*
Faculty and staff continually evaluate the outcomes of their decisions and practices.
Collaboration *(intelligent participation):*
Participants in meetings or conversations are respectful, flexible, informed, and thoughtful.
Execution *(doing small things well):*
School staff are efficient, competent, professional, and responsive.

Table I.6 Connecting the Cultural Dots—Part III

How Do We Achieve Our Vision?

Instructional Systems
 Fully enact five instructional systems: employment, mentoring, curriculum, teacher evaluation, and staff development
 Conform to goals and content of instructional worldview
 Help realize agreed-upon teaching model

Administrative Commitment
 Focuses on instruction
 Participates in training regime
 Has a deep understanding of instructional worldview
 Is adept at conducting instructional conversations
 Regularly employs purposeful approaches to problem-solving
 Reinterprets state/district mandates

Organizational Commitment
 Aligns instructional initiatives with worldview
 Allocates resources in alignment with worldview and components of instructional culture
 Makes regular adjustments to resource allocation
 Includes administrators as participants in implementing instructional initiatives
 Protects instructional time
 Limits number and type of instructional initiatives
 Adapts school routines to goals and content of instructional initiatives

Instructional Discourse
 Honors diverse abilities, talents, and aspirations of student population
 Believes that parents make best efforts to support the goals of schooling
 Demonstrates deep understandings of curriculum and instruction
 Demonstrates deep understandings of contemporary educational research
 Is open to differing models of curriculum and instruction
 Holds deliberate meetings focused on teaching and learning
 Reflects on practice to purposefully approach problem-solving

Doing Small Things Well
 <u>Professional:</u> school staff are dedicated to continuous improvement of knowledge and skills
 <u>Responsive</u>: questions, information, and services are forwarded to the proper offices and personnel
 <u>Competent</u>: school staff are knowledgeable and skillful practitioners
 <u>Efficient</u>: answers, information, and services are provided in a timely manner

Chapter 1

The Goal Maze

> "What is Lewis talking about anyway? I thought we weren't using common core this year. Why can't they just hand out the PowerPoint presentation and let us get into our classrooms?"
>
> (Teacher to Colleague at Opening Day Address)

"Jane, how was your trip to Southeast Asia?"

"Cynthia, it should be on everyone's bucket list. Truly mind-changing. We have to talk about it. Do you have the agenda for today?"

"Same old, same old. You know, new beginnings, new goals, new challenges, and all with fewer materials, fewer personnel, and larger class sizes. Look at the title of Dr. Smith's address: "Meeting Performance Goals." Wasn't that the goal last year?

"No, last year, it was something to do with raising the bar."

"It's dark in here. I'm having trouble reading my class list. Didn't you have Brian Goodlad last year."

"Yes, Brian's a challenge, but if you go along with his sense of humor, he's a great kid."

"What is Lewis talking about anyway? I thought we weren't using common core this year. Why can't they just hand out the PowerPoint presentation and let us get into our classrooms?"

GOAL TRIAGE

Each school year, school administrators and teachers carry into their offices and classrooms a long list of goals that their state, school community, and professional organizations expect them to implement. New York, for example, has one hundred and fifty-one goals, regulating how you lead a school ("shared decision-making"), how you manage a school ("five-year facilities plan"), what you should teach ("library and information skills"), how you should teach ("student calculators"), and the length of the school year ("180 days of instruction"). Added to these formal governmental goals, are goals that a particular school community asks the school to pursue (AP Courses, Work Programs, Extra-Curricular Programs, and College Counseling). At the end of the governmental and community lists of goals, are professional goals originating from university researchers and educational associations ("engage and connect diverse communities to ensure the success of each learner").

Figure 1.1 illustrates the maze of goals that administrators and teachers are asked to navigate each year. The twists and turns of the maze are constructed around goals that are unclear ("love of learning"), goals that contradict each other (standardize/individuate), and goals that are unachievable ("ensure equality"). Each school year, school leaders find themselves thrown into the middle of this maze with the mandate of guiding teachers and students through the maze without fundamentally changing the design or the content of the maze.

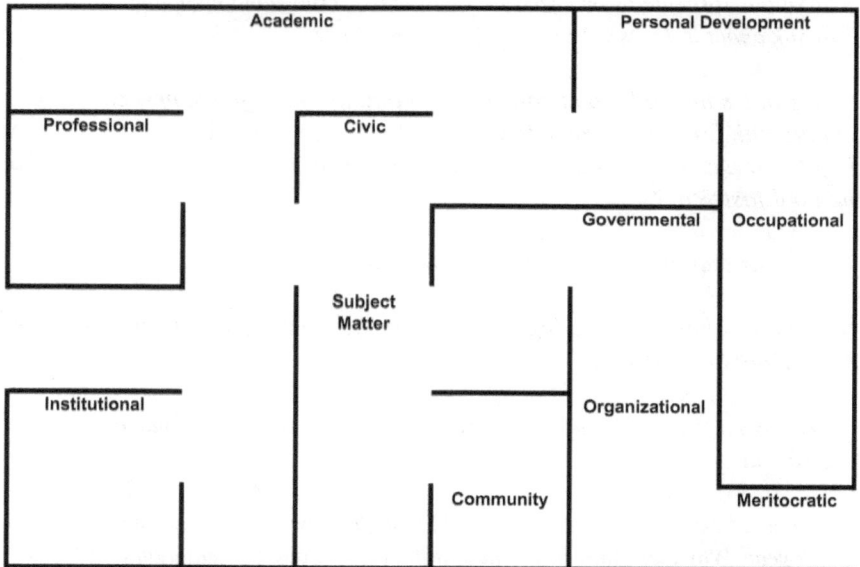

Figure 1.1 The Goal Maze.

School administrators bring some semblance of direction and order inside the maze by the managerial practice of "goal triage" (see table 1.1). Those goals that require a political or institutional response rise to the top ("ASAP" and "PLAN OF ACTION"). Those goals that involve educational or instructional goals—living up to a school's mission statement—are positioned in the "shadows" of political, institutional, organizational and community goals ("SHADOW").

The practice of "goal triage" is on display every month at school board meetings. The first ten minutes of board agendas invite teachers and students to illustrate one or more "shadow" goals in action. Board members and school administrators make the following assumptions while observing the instructional practice:

- *the practice aligns with educational goals listed in the school mission statement,*
- *the practice is grounded in sound learning theories, and*
- *the practice is performed correctly by teachers throughout the building.*

Table 1.1 Goal Triage

TRIAGE LEVEL	SOURCE OF GOAL	TYPE OF GOAL
ASAP (Political and Institutional Goals)	Board of Education Central Office State Accountability Offices State/National Accreditation Schoolwide crises Labor contracts	Budget goals School goals Construction goals Achievement goals Testing mandates Accreditation visit Transportation/food service Safety (e.g., gangs, drugs, guns, and fights) Personnel (e.g., grievances)
Plan of Action (Organizational and Community Goals)	Central Office State Accountability Offices Schoolwide crises Parent concerns	Data management system operations Test-preparation program implementation "100% Graduation Rate Program" implementation Community (e.g., extracurricular activities, advanced course offerings Police Liaison Officer employment New head football coach employment
Shadow (Educational and Instructional Goals)	Board of Education Central Office Professional Organizations Educational research Teachers Administrators	Mission statement goals Board goals (educational) Classroom goals (class size, aides, professional development) Curriculum standards Social justice ideals/goals Lifestyle goals Model instructional strategies

Board members and school administrators rarely question these assumptions governing the shadow goals. Even when a board member or administrator asks an errant question about a shadow goal, the administrative response reduces the complex connection between educational goals and instructional practices—the educational mission of schooling—to simple connections between an assumption and an organizational routine—the managerial mission of schooling:

Board Member to Administrators:

> *"I am concerned that the teaching of math concepts sacrifices the teaching of basic computational skills."*

Administrator to Board Member:

> *"Dr. Jameston, our university math consultant, has assured me that our new math curriculum will provide our students with a firm grounding in basic computational skills."*

The next hour of the school board meeting will be consumed with conversations and votes over political and institutional goals that administrators propose in order to keep schools in the district running smoothly (ASAP goals). Depending on the political or institutional goal in question, administrators take turns presenting the problem or issue they are responsible for: the business manager addresses budget issues, the assistant superintendent for Curriculum and Instruction addresses low achievement scores, the board attorney addresses grievances, the superintendent addresses construction projects, and the appropriate building or central office administrator addresses the crisis of the day. Each administrator employs the same managerial script in presenting a solution to the issue or problem (see figure 1.2).

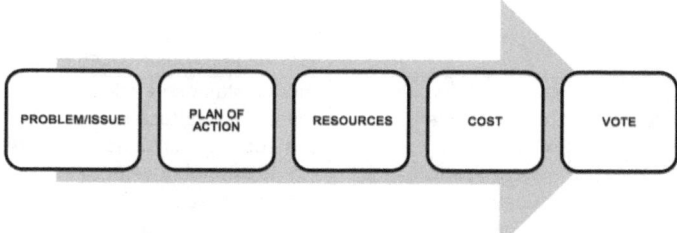

Figure 1.2 The Vote.

While all of the political and institutional issues brought up at board meetings directly or indirectly affect educational goals, administrators seated around the conference table overlook the connections between managerial and educational problems. Even when the problem or issue is clearly educational in nature—low test scores—the plan of action is entirely managerial: purchase a program, employ a consultant, add minutes to the school day, or develop a retention policy.

The remaining half hour of the board meeting invites administrators and board members to express their views and recommendations on problems or issues reflecting their personal interests: extracurricular activities, computers, managerial techniques, prized academic programs, specialty programs, construction, or rules infringing on personal values or behaviors. Similar to the ASAP goals, all "Plan of Action" goals will reference an educational value or goal. When a course of action is agreed upon, the educational goal or value will be displaced by managerial talk of vendors, materials, appearance, specifications, location, and maintenance.

Even when political circumstances force an *educational* goal into the ASAP category, school administrators avoid full implementation of the substance of the goal by assuming one or more managerial roles listed below. Each managerial role is different in tone, staging, and implementation. However, all roles lead to the same outcome: being goalless.

ABSENTEE LANDLORDS

Administrators assuming this role view goal implementation as a matter of announcing and delegating. Goals presented in PowerPoint presentations at the beginning of the school year disappear by Thanksgiving. Goals that become contentious are tabled or compromised away. Goals that appear to be vague, contradictory, or unachievable are left vague, contradictory, and unachievable. The confusion brought on by the comings and goings of poorly implemented goals causes faculty to become distrustful of the worth and execution of schoolwide change initiatives.

TECHNOCRATS

Administrators assuming this role view goal implementation as a matter of designing systems to allocate resources, train teachers, and monitor quantitative measures of student progress. The pressure brought on by the continual monitoring of proper goal implementation causes faculty to deliver shallow representations of schoolwide change initiatives.

BUREAUCRATS

Administrators assuming this role view goal implementation as a matter of documenting compliance with rules and procedures of an announced goal. The bureaucratic goal of proper and timely documentation causes faculty to reduce goal implementation to the single task of sending the right form to the right office.

TRUE BELIEVERS

Administrators assuming this role view goal implementation as a single-minded pursuit of true representations of a theory or technique in classrooms. True believers design elaborate performance-based tools to observe and document the right implementation of instructional theories and techniques. The disconnect between abstract instructional theories and classroom realities causes faculty to engage in various forms of sabotage.

Board agendas filled with political goals, community goals, and organizational goals protect administrators and board members from becoming entangled in the dilemmas, interpretative nightmares, and difficult prioritization built into any maze-like goal structure. In return for managerial scripts that keep schools running smoothly, administrators forfeit the opportunity to translate the yearly maze of goals into a commonly understood vision of schooling—the shadow goals of schooling. Without a coherent and practical understanding of the shadow goals of schooling, administrators, teachers, parents, and students become helpless wanderers in an ever-expanding maze of goals.

> *When you have the Superintendent show up to a curriculum-writing project, you know this goal is not going away soon.*
>
> *Teacher to Colleague at Opening Day Address*

"Jane, how was your trip to Southeast Asia?"

"Cynthia, it should be on everyone's bucket list. Truly mind-changing. We have to talk about it."

"Well, you know what I did this summer? I volunteered for that curriculum-writing project. The pay was good, but what a grind. Our consultant really knew her stuff, but she was also very demanding. She kept us writing for three hours each day. Dr. Smith sat with us the entire time."

"Did you finish the project?"

"Yes, we did. The consultant is doing a final edit, but we will see the finished project next week."

"What do you think about it?"

"It certainly changes how we present content. There is a real emphasis on discussion—what the consultant called 'academic discussion.' Although I became interested in writing the scenarios and problems that begin each class, I am a bit uneasy about how I would conduct one of these discussions. You remember that seventh period class I had two years ago? I can't imagine how that group would take to listening to other students' viewpoints, providing evidence for their opinions, and questioning facts. That is all going to be part of the training we receive this year, but I still can't see myself doing these lessons well."

"Well, I agree with the goals of the project, but you are right, I can't see our students doing an academic discussion."

"I would say this: based on what Dr. Smith said in our curriculum writing sessions, the district is fully committed to providing whatever resources we need to integrate this program into our daily lessons. When you have the Superintendent show up to a curriculum-writing project, you know this goal is not going away soon."

THE PROPER VETTING OF SCHOOL GOALS

The architecture of the goal maze is constructed around a compliance mindset: implement the goals established by local and national governmental bodies—ASAP and Plan of Action goals. Without a mindset conditioned to assess the value of a mandated goal, school administrators are unable to lead their faculties out of the twists and turns of whatever governmental bodies toss into main office in-boxes. Trapped in the maze, managerial mindsets establish organizational and instructional routines designed to document their movements in the maze. Moving back and forth in the maze gives rise to the most frequent opening day comment made by teachers: "didn't we do this last year?"

School administrators with an educational mindset author a process for questioning the purposes, worth, and feasibility of each goal that enters main offices. Figure 1.3 illustrates the process that educational mindsets would initiate when considering what goals will be pursued in the coming school year. Each question in the vetting process must be answered in the affirmative before proceeding to the next question.

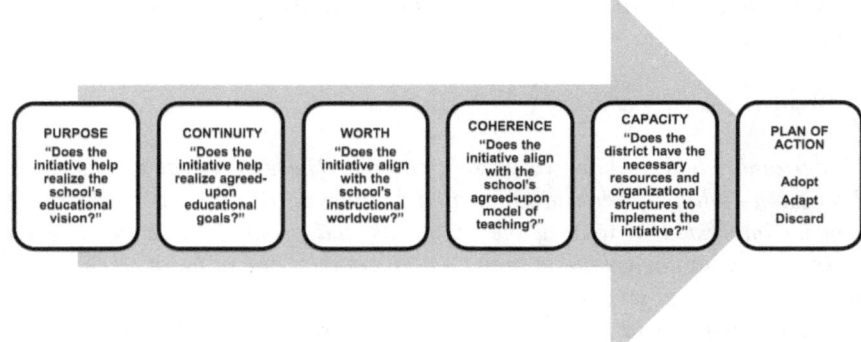

Figure 1.3   Vetting a School Goal.

No vetting process is free of the institutional realities of schooling. School administrators grapple with the institutional goals of schooling by adjusting their plans of action to accommodate the value or goal they are being asked to implement. On a continuum of strategies for goal implementation, school administrators design plans of actions that align with the answers to the questions in the vetting process. If the answers to the questions in the vetting process are yes, the initiative becomes fixed in the school's organizational and instructional routines (ADOPT). If only some of the answers are yes, the school administrator reinterprets the initiative, modifying it to be in line with established organizational and instructional routines (ADAPT). If the goal is in opposition to the school's educational vision—the answers are no to the questions in the vetting process—the school administrator complies with the form, but not the substance of the goal (DISCARD).

STANDING GOAL TRIAGE ON ITS HEAD

The goal maze that administrators, teachers, and students enter each year is a predictable outcome of a managerial mindset focused on the efficient implementation of mandates, laws, programs, and initiatives delivered to main office in-boxes. Without a clear, compelling, and feasible vision of schooling—why are we here—the goals rising to the top of main office in-boxes are ones that are easily managed: add a resource, write a policy, redesign a system, employ personnel, or adopt a program. The goals falling to the bottom of main office in-boxes are ones that are difficult to enact. They require developing collective understandings and applications of the abstractions of school mission statements: critical thinking, effective communication, collaborative teamwork, thinking across disciplinary cultures, and flexible thinkers.

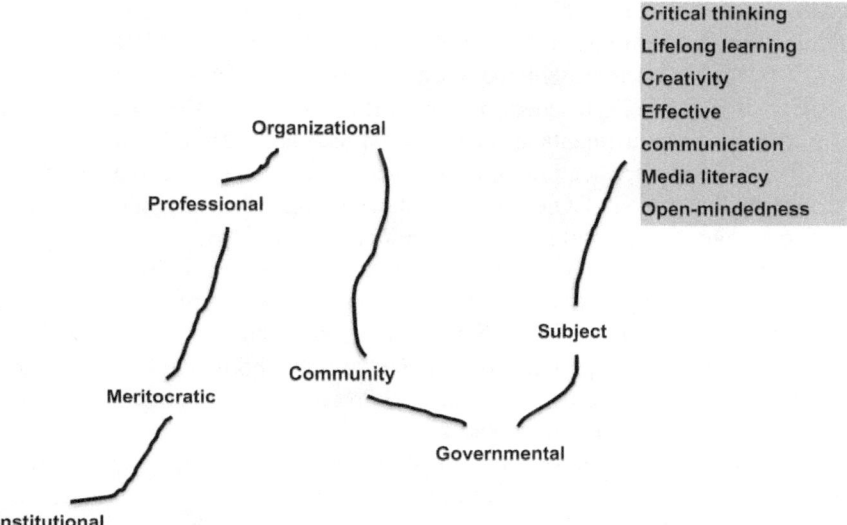

Figure 1.4 Educational Roadmap.

An educational mindset turns goal triage on its head: shadow goals become ASAP goals and Plan of Action and ASAP goals become shadow goals. Each educational goal listed in school mission statements now becomes a valued end of schooling, not a means to an institutional or political end. Standing the goal triage on its head reorients the direction and operation of schools: goal mazes become roadmaps (see figure 1.4) and organizational and instructional routines help realize educational outcomes (see Resource 1–1).

WHY AM I HERE?

The set of goals that school leaders decide to pursue depends on how they answer the question: why am I here? (see Resource 1-2). Those with managerial mindsets believe the primary function of school administrators is to document the implementation of the policies, procedures, and mandates contained in the teacher packets handed out on opening day. This managerial process consists of three administrative functions: telling, allocating, and inspecting. Resources 1-3, 1-4, 1-5, and 1-6 represent the vocabularies and processes school managers employ to TELL teachers what goals they will be pursuing; to describe the resources that will be ALLOCATED to achieve those goals; and to describe the process that will be employed to INSPECT the achievement of these goals.

Those with educational mindsets believe the primary function of school administrators is to help faculty make collective sense out of the educational goals listed in school mission statements. This process consists of three administrative functions: educating, facilitating, and coaching. Resources 1-7, 1-8, 1-9, and 1-10 represent the vocabularies and processes school leaders employ to EDUCATE teachers on the worth of the goals they will be pursuing; to describe adjustments to the organizational and instructional routines to FACILITATE the application of these goals; and to identify the role the administrators will assume in COACHING understandings of these goals in practice.

The managerial functions of telling, allocating and inspecting solve *technical problems*. School administrators with a managerial mindset spend their office hours making certain that fixed organizational routines are followed. Teachers spend their classroom hours making sure that instructional routines are followed. In this managerial mindset model, both administrators and teachers spend their preparation times documenting compliance with organizational and instructional routines.

The educational functions of teaching, facilitating, and coaching solve *relational problems*. School administrators with an educational mindset spend their days in teacher work areas assisting teachers with developing the connections between goals (e.g., "critical thinking," "caring and collaborative learning community," or "where learning is exciting") and the types of instructional experiences best suited for achieving these goals. Teachers spend their days in classrooms experimenting with the right mix of instructional experiences to place students in situations where they are thinking critically, are engaging in collective sensemaking, and are excited about learning. In this educational mindset model, both administrators and teachers spend their preparation time critiquing the connections between educational goals and teaching practices.

The set of goals that a school administrator decides to pursue determines the values, beliefs, and practices that the school community will participate in for the coming school year. The pursuit of managerial goals of schooling—mandates, laws, initiatives, directives, and programs—places administrators, teachers, and students squarely the middle of the goal maze with no road map to guide them out. The pursuit of educational goals of schooling—curriculum design, models of teaching, and supervisory roles—places administrators, teachers, and students at the entrance to the maze with a road map to guide them out. Perhaps more importantly, it gives administrators the instructional tools to achieve the goals that attracted teachers and administrators to the teaching profession.

RESOURCES

RESOURCE 1-1: What Goals Should We Pursue?

	INSTITUTIONAL ENDS	EDUCATIONAL ENDS	
Goals	Accountability Compliance Status Funding Control	Problem-solving Creativity Effective communication Media literacy Critical thinking Open-mindedness	
Structure	Success or failure is independent of others Hierarchical (teacher-controlled)	Classrooms (Rows-30 desks) Seat-time Periods Subjects Credits Grades	Performance depends on others Teacher as facilitator Teamwork Self-directed Interdisciplinary Problem-based Thematic	Workrooms/labs Multipurpose rooms Academic clusters Media centers
Tasks	Information recall Application of standard formulae Recitation No assistance from technology learning tools	Note-taking Worksheets Chalkboard Overhead Projector PowerPoint Quizzes Tests	Interpretation of information Application of appropriate explanatory framework Performances Appropriate technologies	Media centers Labs Information/databases Industry-wide technologies and resources Mentoring/apprenticeships
Content	Fixed body of knowledge Facts and processes detached from meaningful context Contrived school/academic problems	Teacher-directed Textbooks Worksheets Standardized testing	Long-distance learning Simulations Computer modeling Interactive technology	Contingent body of knowledge Facts and processes are situation-specific Real-world problems

RESOURCE 1-2: Why am I here?

WHY, WHAT, HOW	FUNCTIONS
Why am I here?	To manage or to lead? To be an instructional manager or instructional leader? To prepare young people or to educate young people?
What do I control?	Instructional worldview Instructional systems School discourse Administrative focus Organizational capacity
What is important?	Valued ends of schooling (and gaps between these and classroom realities) Social, emotional, and intellectual development of young people Creating a culture of continuous learning
What do I know?	What is my philosophy of teaching and learning? What theories, concepts, ideas, and practices make up this philosophy? What method of inquiry would I employ to resolve an instructional problem?
How do I implement?	How do I organize my school to achieve the valued ends of schooling? What resources will I need to achieve the valued ends of schooling? Does my staff possess the knowledge and skills to achieve the valued ends of schooling?

RESOURCE 1-3: Memo from Superintendent to Central Office Staff: Board Goals

COMMUNITY HIGH SCHOOL DISTRICT 108

MEMORANDUM

To: B. Smith, K. Louis, F. Daley, M. Johnson, L. Zimmer

From: C. Franklyn

Subject: Board Goals

As you know, at our strategic planning retreat this summer, the Board identified thirty-two goals for the coming school year. Bill has developed an accountability matrix that we will use to inform the Board of our progress on each goal. Attached to this memorandum is a list of Board goals, the administrator in charge of monitoring the goal(s), and a calendar indicating when progress reports will be due. Our staff has designed all the forms that will be required to report progress on goal achievement. At our weekly team meeting, please bring possible templates we might adopt to monitor the goals you have been assigned. The templates you design should meet the following criteria:

- Measurable outcomes
- Data format is compatible with the district data management software
- Data is valid, reliable, and can be collected in a timely manner
- Data collected can be understood by non-specialists

RESOURCE 1-4: Memo from Superintendent to Principals: Board Goals

COMMUNITY HIGH SCHOOL DISTRICT 108

MEMORANDUM

To: All Principals

From: C. Franklyn

Subject: Board Goal Documents

Attached is a packet of forms the Board has approved to evaluate progress on the goals established at this year's strategic planning retreat. I have also included a calendar listing the due dates for completion of the forms, a description of how the forms should be completed, and samples of fully completed accountability forms. I cannot stress enough the importance of the accurate and timely reporting of data listed on these forms. If you have any questions regarding the completion of these forms contact Bill Levy, in Data, Assessment, and Research.

RESOURCE 1-5: Memo from Principal to Teachers: Data Management Calendar

COMMUNITY HIGH SCHOOL DISTRICT 108

MEMORANDUM

To: All Faculty

From: A. Smith, Principal

Subject: Data Management Calendar

Attached is a calendar listing key dates regarding the forms contained in your opening day information packets. As announced at our opening institute day, the accurate and timely return of these forms will allow the District Director of Accountability to comply with all board and school improvement goals.

Due to the wide discrepancies we found in last year's learning growth data, the district has employed a consultant to train teachers to accurately complete the forms contained in your information packets. The attached calendar shows the dates of these training sessions as well as the dates that the completed forms are due.

RESOURCE 1-6: Opening Day Agenda: Meeting Performance Goals

	WELCOME BACK	
8:00–8:30	Coffee and Rolls	Cafeteria
8:30–9:00	Message from the Superintendent *"Excellence is a Tradition"*	Thomason Auditorium
9:00–9:30	Message from the Principal *"Meeting Performance Goals"*	
9:30–11:30	Dr. Susan Johnson *"Data-Driven Teaching"*	
11:30–12:30	LUNCH	Cafeteria
12:30–1:30	Dr. Susan Johnson *"What did we learn today?"*	Thomason Auditorium
1:30–2:30	Dr. Ernest Wilson *"How to Collect and Report Data in the Classroom"*	
2:30–3:00	Content Area Team Meetings *"Curriculum Mapping"*	Team Meeting Rooms
3:00	Dismissal	

RESOURCE 1-7: Memo from Superintendent to Central Office Staff: Board Goals

COMMUNITY HIGH SCHOOL DISTRICT 108

MEMORANDUM

To: B. Smith, K. Louis, F. Daley, M. Johnson, L. Zimmer

From: C. Franklyn

Subject: Board Goals

As you know, at our strategic planning retreat last summer, the Board agreed to support the development of a freshman interdisciplinary program and funded curriculum-writing projects in core academic subjects. Each of you has been assigned specific responsibilities for the implementation of these two district goals.

At our next education committee meeting, please be ready to provide board members with a brief progress report on each district goal. These progress reports should contain:

- Goals of curriculum-writing projects and our interdisciplinary program "C3,"
- Templates used to write curriculum and representative samples of completed curriculum projects, and
- Program design for the C3 program: goals, subjects, teachers selected for program, selection criteria for students, schedule, grading/assessment templates, sample unit of instruction, and timelines for final implementation.

At the end of week, Ruth will give you times when we can get together individually to review your report. If possible, I would like one teacher from the new interdisciplinary program to be present at the meeting.

RESOURCE 1-8: Memo from Superintendent to Principals: Board Goals

COMMUNITY HIGH SCHOOL DISTRICT 108

MEMORANDUM

To: All Principals

From: C. Franklyn

Subject: Board Goals

At our next education committee meeting, Central Office staff will provide a progress report on our curriculum-writing projects and the design of our interdisciplinary program. I am asking those principals involved in piloting the curriculum-writing projects and interdisciplinary program to attend the meeting. I am not expecting any formal reports. Be prepared, however, to answer any logistical questions about the implementation of both board goals. Please contact me directly if you have any questions regarding the meeting. I want to thank you in advance for both assisting Central Office personnel with the organizational changes required to implement both goals and, most importantly, your commitment to the educational goals we established two years ago.

RESOURCE 1-9: Memo from Principal to Teachers: Pilot Programs

COMMUNITY HIGH SCHOOL DISTRICT 108

MEMORANDUM

To: All Faculty

From: A. Smith, Principal

Subject: Pilot Programs

As you know, we have had teams of teachers involved in rewriting curricula in mathematics and social studies. The goal of these curriculum rewrites was to design content, activity structures and assessments that would align with Deborah Meier's five habits of thought. In addition to this project, four teachers in our building have designed a freshman interdisciplinary program. I have asked representatives from both projects to present a brief description of the process and outcomes of each project.

Programs aimed at reaching these board goals will be piloted in our school. Our ultimate goal is for these programs to become schoolwide practices. To effectively incorporate these programs, we have designed opportunities for the faculty to provide feedback on the content and teaching practices of each project. These feedback sessions will be led by Ms. Anna McCarthy, our university liaison. Again, I would like to thank all faculty who have contributed their time and expertise to creating these two valuable additions to our instructional program.

RESOURCE 1-10: Opening Day Agenda: Living Up to our School's Mission Statement

	WELCOME BACK	
8:00–8:30	Coffee and Rolls	Cafeteria
8:30–9:30	Message from the Superintendent *"Living Up to our School's Mission Statement"*	Thomason Auditorium
	Message from the Principal *"Central High's Instructional Worldview"*	
9:30–10:00	B. Sanders, G. Livingston, G. Cole *Project Report: Curriculum Rewrites*	
10:00–11:00	D. Smith, S. Owens, L. Parks *Project Report: Interdisciplinary Program*	
11:00–11:30	Dr. Anna McCarthy *"Habits of Mind & Assessment"*	
11:30–12:30	LUNCH	Cafeteria
12:30–1:30	Team Meetings	Thomason Auditorium
1:30–3:00	Individual Classroom Preparation	
3:00	Dismissal	

Chapter 2

Championing

> *"I'm in the middle of budgets, that EPA complaint, and getting the new data processing package up and running. Alright, ask Jeff to stop by and brief me on the interdisciplinary program."*
>
> *(Principal to Secretary)*

"Jane, what does my day look like?"

"You have a strategic planning meeting at 10 at the District Office. The folder on your desk has the agenda for the meeting.

You have the Lions Club meeting at 12. The plaque for student of the month has already been delivered to the restaurant.

You are meeting with Dr. James at Central High South at 2."

"You are chairing the PTA meeting at 3:30 to discuss the new interdisciplinary program."

"I asked Jeff to chair that meeting. He developed the program."

"Yes, I know. Jeff is certainly excited about the program. But the Superintendent wants you to lead the meeting."

"Just what I need now. I'm in the middle of budgets, that EPA complaint, and getting the new data processing package up and running. Alright, ask Jeff to stop by and brief me on the interdisciplinary program."

WHAT KIND OF ORGANIZATION AM I LEADING?

What do school administrators see each day when they walk through hallways, peer into classrooms, chair meetings, and review daily calendars? Students sitting in classrooms *managing* institutional goals: assignments, grades, and credits. Teachers standing in front of classrooms *managing* institutional goals: attendance, curriculum guides, and grade books. Administrators seated in offices *managing* institutional goals: budgets, personnel, schedules, and mandates. Even the factory-style architecture of most schools is designed to *manage* institutional goals: controlling the movement and credentialing of student populations. None of these institutional goals are designed to create learning environments conducive to the types of outcomes listed in school mission statements: lifelong learners, critical thinkers, and effective communicators.

Organizations designed to *control* behavior assume the populations they serve enter workspaces from nowhere: that the performance of these blank slates is wholly dependent upon the structure of the organization and the type of incentive system adopted to motivate individuals to act in the best interest of the organization. The mindsets of controlling schools employ a mix of rewards, sanctions, rules, and inspection to "motivate" teachers and students to conform to institutional goals and values.

Organizations designed to *liberate* behavior assume the populations, they serve enter workspaces from somewhere: that the performance of these agents is wholly dependent on accommodating and expanding upon the individual interests, abilities, and understandings of the populations they serve. The mindsets of liberating schools employ a mix of choice, inquiry, expertise, usefulness, and feedback to inspire teachers and students to pursue more deeply an interest or a talent (see table 2.1).

Managerial mindsets are most comfortable with managing architectures of control: goals are mandated, processes are prescribed, and outcomes are measured. Educational mindsets are most comfortable with designing architectures of liberation: goals are self-determined, processes are contingent, and outcomes are reached. Managerial mindsets enter main offices to enforce policy and procedural regimes that achieve the goal of institutional schooling: conformity. Educational mindsets enter main offices to promote a set of values and practices that achieve the goal of becoming educated: agency.

MANAGING, LEADING, AND CHAMPIONING

A persistent theme in all school mission statements is empowering the diverse talents, abilities, and interests of their student bodies. Although this educational value is a staple of opening day administrative speeches, main

Table 2.1 What Is the Mindset of Your Organization?

ATTRIBUTES	MINDSET OF CONTROL (Bureaucrats)	MINDSET OF LIBERATION (Champions)
Goals	• Efficiency • Certainty • Conformity	• Creativity • Innovation • Flexibility
Culture	• Hierarchy: Top-down decision-making	• Flat structure and egalitarian culture
Occupational Roles	• Position in a hierarchy • Prescribed responsibilities and functions (Job Descriptions)	• Expertise • Particular requirements to complete a task (Task Specifications)
Organizational Environments	• Impersonal • Roles and position in chain of command • Discourse focused on efficiently implementing rules and procedures	• Interpersonal • Professionalism and autonomy • Discourse focused on solving problems
Documentation	• A priority • Codification of rules, procedures and institutional decision-making	• A nuisance • Journals, notebooks, scraps of paper, chalkboards documenting relationships between theories and practice
Accountability	• Analysis of data • Sanctions for noncompliance • Benchmarks • Alignment with rules and procedures • Standardized measures of achievement	• Observation of intentional states (beliefs, satisfactions, feelings, judgment) • Reflection on practice • Level of thinking • Methods of inquiry • Performance on real-world tasks
Vocabularies	• Must • Should • Ought to • Need to	• Can • Could • Consider • Might
Response of Teachers and Students	• Resistance/oppositional behavior • Going through the motions ("doing school," "doing a job") • Passivity	• Assuming responsibility • Going beyond competence • Enthusiasm

Table 2.2 Three Roles of School Administration

ROLE	PROCESS	TASKS
What Managers Do (Implement)	Tell→allocate→inspect	Standardize Schedule Allocate Follow-up
What Leaders Do (Direct)	Plan→facilitate→build capacity	Organize Model Monitor Redesign
What Champions Do (Author)	Disrupt→purpose→enact	Challenge Purpose Educate Authorize

offices rely heavily on organizational and institutional structures that marginalize instructional programs that would unleash the diverse talents, abilities, and interests of their student bodies. Managerial mindsets view empowerment as a threat to the certainties of established organizational and instructional routines. Educational mindsets view all forms of control as a threat to the educational goals and values listed in school mission statements.

Resolving the dilemma between the certainties of control and the disruptions of empowerment involves the skillful navigation of the three roles of school administration: *managing, leading,* and *championing* (see table 2.2). Administrators must take into account the local circumstances of their schools as they determine the right mix of the certainties of management, the coherency of leadership, and the creativity of championing. Each administrative role is vital: without certainty, schools become unsafe; without coherency, schools become confused; and without creativity, schools become stagnant.

> "Jane, I set up an earlier meeting with Dr. Wilson. I need to explain why I didn't check all the boxes on the county form."
>
> *(Principal to Secretary)*

"Jane, what does my day look like?"

> "You have a post-conference meeting at 8 with Mrs. James. Your script notes are in your observation file.
>
> At 9 and 10 you are observing Mr. Townsend and then Mrs. Rhodes. Mrs. Rhodes has seen me twice about the observation. She is a bit nervous about it. It's her first teaching position and her first observation.

At 2 you have a meeting with the Regional Superintendent at the county office. I put two copies of the school improvement plan in the other folder on your desk. Is this wrong? The letter from the Regional Superintendent indicated that all the principals are handing in their plans at a 3:00 meeting."

"I set up an earlier meeting with Dr. Wilson. I need to explain why I didn't check all the boxes on the county form.

And Jane, I won't be coming back to the office after the regional meeting. I made an appointment with Dr. Hernandez, the bilingual coordinator at Yorktown. Mrs. Gomez gave me an opinion piece he wrote in the local newspaper describing the same problems we are having with our program."

CHAMPIONING A MATHEMATICAL VISION

How would managers, leaders, and champions approach a real-world instructional problem: the adoption of new standards in mathematics? In main offices occupied by managers and leaders, they would view the adoption of new standards in mathematics as a problem of implementation. The managerial and leadership functions perfectly align with the tasks of implementation: presenting, distributing, training, and inspecting (see table 2.3).

Champions view the managerial tasks of implementation as the last step in a process designed to determine the worth of adapting new standards in mathematics. The logistics of handing out materials, scheduling half-day workshops, and purchasing data collection technologies, become secondary to the valued-added questions of merit and meaning:

- Do the new standards help realize the educational values and goals of the school's mission statement? (see Resource 2-1),
- How will the educational values and goals endorsed by the new standards be communicated to the school community? (see Resource 2-2, 2-3), and
- How will teachers make collective sense out of the theories and practices promoted by the new standards? (see Resource 2-4, 2-5).

Table 2.3 Implementing

TASK	AUDIENCE	RESPONSIBILITY	TOOLS	GOAL
Presentation	Faculty	Assistant Superintendent	PowerPoint	Adoption
Distribution of Materials	Teachers	Principal	Guides and Training Schedules	Implementation
Training	Teachers	Consultant	Schedules and Forms	Compliance
Inspection	Principals and Teachers	Assistant Superintendent	Goals, Schedules, and Forms	Accountability

Answering each valued-added question involves the weaving together of the four distinct functions of championing a new instructional initiative: purposing, educating, strategizing, and implementing. Table 2.4 summarizes the first three of these. When determining how to enact these functions, a champion must consider the math background of faculty and students, the current math program, the organization of the school, the support of the principal, the quality of professional development programs, available school resources, and the school community's expectations. While managers and leaders pay little attention to the purposing process, champions view each function as a means of offering teachers a new pedagogical model that appeals to their sense of mission, their authority to interpret theories and practices, and their professional goal of advancing their craft knowledge.

Common Core Standards in Mathematics (CCSM) serves as a perfect vehicle for infusing the educational goals and values of school mission statements into daily classroom lessons. To fully achieve the educational mission of CCSM, school administrators must orchestrate the implementation function of a manager, the facilitation function of the leader, and the purposing function of the champion. Without the championing function, managerial and leadership functions would marginalize the goals and practices of CCSM. School administrators who assume the role of champion must step out of the traditional trajectories of their managerial colleagues and step into the trajectory that readies them to become strong champions of the schools' mission statements.

Table 2.4 Championing

TASK	ASSESSING THE INITIATIVE
Purposing	WILL this initiative help realize a valued end of schooling? DOES this initiative align with our school's instructional worldview? DOES this initiative contain familiar theories and practices? WILL the district support this initiative?
Educating	WHY are we pursuing this initiative? WHAT makes this initiative distinctive? WHAT theories, ideas, and practices govern this initiative? HOW does this initiative fit into what we are already doing? WHAT organizational changes will we need to implement to accommodate this initiative?
Strategizing	WHAT are the desired outcomes of this initiative? WHAT instructional systems will need to be redesigned to accommodate this initiative? WHAT organizational routines will need to be redesigned to accommodate this initiative? WHAT measurements will be tracked to assess progress in implementing this initiative? WHAT organizational resources will be needed to support this initiative? WHAT role will I play in implementing this initiative?

BECOMING A STRONG CHAMPION

There are two formidable obstacles to school administrators becoming champions: one is institutional; the other is personal. The institutional obstacle is that the very nature of advancement in educational careers creates managerial administrators. Newly employed school administrators enter main offices composed of layers of beliefs, organizational structures, and managerial practices designed to accomplish institutional goals—standardization, implementation, and documentation. School administrators intent on rising up through the ranks in main and central offices fill their resumes with managerial and leadership tasks that showcase their ability to effectively and efficiently accomplish institutional tasks: balance budgets, create schedules, complete ambitious building projects, mollify special interest concerns, pass referendums, write technology plans, and implement new software programs. None of these managerial tasks move classroom teaching toward the educational goals and values written into school mission statements, but they are tasks that guarantee the rapid and certain advancement of careers in school administration.

For administrators deciding to become champions, the first stage in this transformation is to place the managerial and leadership roles of school administration in their proper place. Successfully implementing educational goals and values listed in school mission statements requires paying attention to managerial and leadership tasks. These tasks, however, are not sufficient to internalize those goals and values in the hearts, minds, and practices of teachers.

With the admission that managerial tasks alone are poorly suited for connecting a valued end of schooling to a particular mandate, program, or pedagogy, school administrators are left facing the personal obstacle to becoming a strong educational champion: developing an educational persona. This chapter summarizes the fundamental attributes for becoming a *Strong School Champion*. (*Becoming a Strong Instructional Leader: Saying NO to Business as Usual,* provides a more in-depth study of the kinds of formal and informal training that a school administrator would have to undertake in order to develop the pedagogical knowledge and skills to champion the goals and values listed in school mission statements.)

Formal Training

The essential function of championing is the ability to transform abstract educational theories and concepts into the daily activity structures of classrooms: aligning the *what, why,* and *how* of a new instructional initiative. Managers and leaders begin the implementation process with the assumption that the *what* and *why* of an instructional initiative have already been established: the *what* is the mandate; the *why* is a governmental or central office directive. With these assumptions in place, school administrators proceed directly to the *how*: managerial functions of telling, allocating, and inspecting. Certification programs for school administrators validate the managerial leap over the *what* and *why* with course structures heavily populated with the *how* of implementation—finance, law, administration, public relations, and human resources. There are very few elective courses devoted to the *what* and *why* of schooling—history, sociology, philosophy, curriculum, and instruction.

Champions, on the other hand, view the *what* and *why* as an essential first step in implementing a new instructional initiative. All school communities are composed of different segments of the community—parents, teachers, administrators, and students—who are pursuing different sets of goals. Each segment of the community expects that their set of goals will become a priority. The answers to the *what* and *why* questions determine which goals become a priority and how those goals conform to a school's instructional worldview.

To identify and enact the links between goals, values, and practice, a school administrator must have engaged in an eclectic mix of reading about, talking about, and thinking about the fundamental questions of schooling:

- *What are the goals of schooling?*
- *How do children learn?*
- *What knowledge is of most worth?*
- *How should knowledge be organized?*
- *How should we assess what students understand?*
- *How should we teach?*

The goal of these ongoing public conversations and private deliberations—this educative stage of becoming a champion—is to develop a personalized instructional worldview—a coherent response to the fundamental questions of schooling. Resource 2-6 compares two common instructional worldviews. Each worldview sets the stage for what teaching model a school will adopt and how a school will be organized to support that model. Without a well-articulated instructional worldview, main offices, and classrooms become trapped between mandates prescribing one set of goals and values and organizational and classroom practices designed to implement opposing goals and values.

CCSM, for example, clearly embraces the educational goals and values written into most school mission statements: "critical thinking skills," "well prepared for college and career pathways," and "highest educational standards." The successful integration of these goals and values into daily classroom practice would involve adopting a philosophy of teaching and learning closely aligned to *Instructional Worldview B* and a teaching model representing the pedagogical goals and instructional strategies composing a school's agreed-upon model of teaching (see Resource 2-7).

Administrators who choose to bypass the educative stage of champions lack the intellectual tools to shape the process for making collective sense out of CCSM or shape the organizational conditions necessary for applying CCSM in daily classroom instruction. Lacking an authoritative and coherent *what* and *why* of a new instructional initiative, teachers see little reason to adopt pedagogies opposed to how they believe mathematics should be taught.

Confronted with faculties openly hostile to teaching models they do not understand or value, school administrators fall back to a managerial fixation on the inspection function of the implementation process: developing evaluative and data gathering instruments designed to catch teacher resistance to program goals and practices. The fixation on inspection transforms an educative process—*what* and *why* of CCSM—into an instrumental process—documenting compliance with symbolic representations of CCSM.

The Classroom Muddle

Each day, teachers enter their classrooms with the complex job of making collective sense out of diverse student interests, abstract subject matters, the technique of the day, accountability mandates, and parent feedback. In the midst of making sense of the muddle of in-school and out-of-school variables that are often vague, contradictory, and transitory, teachers must be ready to adjust daily instructional routines in response to a whole host of schoolwide and classroom diversions that appear and disappear on a daily basis: student sickness, Friday's pep assembly, malfunctioning technology, fire drills, bomb scares, administrator evaluations, and state testing programs.

It is no surprise then, that theories, concepts, and practices of a new instructional initiative become compromised in schools where out-of-control variables continually disrupt the best-laid plans of teachers. It takes years of experience juggling these school variables to develop a sense of what teachers can understand and apply in their classrooms and what theories and practices extend classroom instruction beyond the *Zone of Practicality* (see Resource 2-8).

Administrative and Supervisory Experiences

The education and training regimes of school administrators lead them to prefer the certainties of managing projects and systems over the uncertainties of educating teachers and students. This managerial bias in main offices treats every new instructional initiative as essentially a problem of properly applying the tasks and functions of administration (see table 2.5). The goal of these

Table 2.5   Administrating CCSM

MANAGING	IMPLEMENTING
Develop goals/objectives	Personnel assignments
Develop policies, procedures, schedules, flowcharts, and job descriptions	Workflow patterns
	Communication flow networks
	Resource assignments
Develop budgets	Measurements
Develop assessment indicators	Data analysis
Establish patterns of authority and responsibility	Systems adjustments based on measurements and data
Acquire necessary materials	Assessment of newly developed policies, procedures, and flowcharts

administrative processes is to *implement* the instructional mandates arriving at the beginning of the school year: presenting the program, distributing materials, scheduling training sessions, documenting classroom behaviors, administering assessment instruments, and analyzing assessment results.

Champions would view the CCSM mandate as an opportunity to transform the way teachers and students think about and perform mathematics. Moving from *implementing* the rules, routines, and practices of a new mandate to *enacting* the goals, theories, and practices of a new instructional methodology (see Resource 2-9) involves a set of skills and processes normally assigned to supervisory personnel (see table 2.6).

Table 2.6   Supervising CCSM

EDUCATING (see Resource 2-5)	FACILITATING (see Resource 2-4)
• Educate:	• Instructional Systems: *aligned with school's instructional worldview (mission statement)*
• *purpose→frame→interpret→leverage→ allocate*	
• Model:	• Administrative Commitment: *deep understanding→problem-solving→participation*
• *observe→expert performance*	
• Practice:	• Organizational Commitment: *resource alignment→adoption of school routines→instructional time protected*
• *perform→feedback*	
• Coach:	
• *mentor→feedback→gaps→discussions →practice*	• Instructional Discourse: *honors diversity→additive (not subtractive) →research based→deliberate meetings*
• Author:	
• *school context→ experience→construct*	
• Standardize:	
• *teaching methods→normalize*	

Champions make a purposeful effort in their career choices to be comfortable in both the administrative world of implementing and the supervisory world of educating. Working in the *administrative world,* champions perform in offices housed in well-established bureaucratic structures. Working in the *supervisory world,* champions admit that these offices are ill-suited for providing teachers with the time, space, materials, and training they will require to abandon comfortable teaching practices and adopt uncomfortable teaching practices.

Working in both worlds, champions use a unique mix of administrative and supervisory skills to create a comfortable fit between bureaucratic structures and educational goals. Table 2.7 summarizes how that comfortable fit looks in practice. Each bureaucratic function is tailored to accommodate the goals and methods of CCSM. The tailoring process involves the supervisory functions of the *what* and *why* of a new instructional initiative and, at the same time, the administrative functions of *how* the *what* and *why* will be achieved within established institutional structures.

Achieving the right balance between theory, classroom practice, and institutional structures is a continual process of shifting between answering *what, why,* and *how* questions (see figure 2.1). The ultimate goal of this collective sensemaking process is to craft a strategy that aligns the educational goals and practices of CCSM with daily classroom lessons in mathematics.

Table 2.7   Finding the Right Fit

SYSTEMS	BUREAUCRATIC (Implementing)	EDUCATIONAL (Enacting)
Budgets	All staff development monies must be funded from approved grants	The district will increase monies for staff development to accommodate training for CCSM
Schedules	Use three five-hour days for CCSM workshops	Redesign master schedule to accommodate common team meeting times
Personnel	Delegate responsibility for materials distribution and workshop scheduling to the assistant superintendent for Curriculum and Instruction	Employ a full-time subject matter coach
Space	Staff development held in classrooms on a rotating basis	Dedicated room in building for staff development
Materials	District mandates that all schools in the district adopt state-approved CCSM curriculum and training materials	District gives schools the discretion to adapt state-approved curriculum materials to local circumstances
Calendar	Two of four teacher institute days will be devoted to CCSM training	All teacher institute days will be devoted to CCSM training

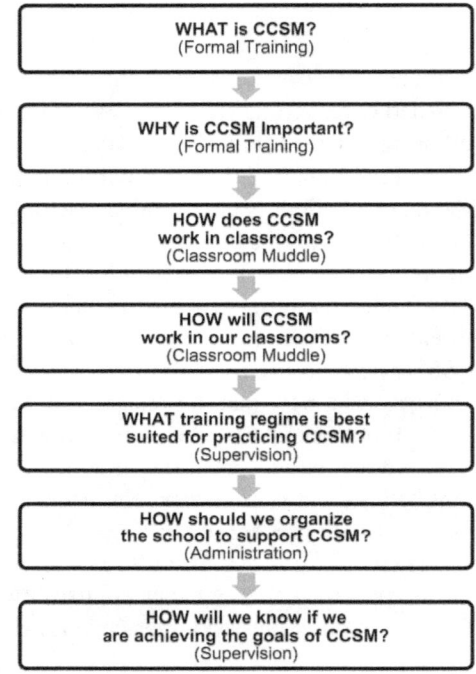

Figure 2.1   Translating Mission into Practice.

WORKING IN THE MARGINS OF SCHOOL ORGANIZATIONS

The educational goals and values written into all school mission statements honor the life of the intellectual mind: a set of skills that develop in young people a sense of intellectual independence (agency); the habit of questioning received wisdom (critical thinking); and the openness to exploring the limits of ideas (impartiality). With this vision of schooling in place, school administrators become intellectual workers guided by the same habits of mind expected of their students: agency, skepticism, and appraisal. Most school administrators sit in main offices *voicing* the life of the intellectual mind, but *practicing* the life of institutions. The habits of the institutional mind—standardization, compliance, and documentation—are in direct opposition to the life of the intellectual mind.

While both visions of schooling surface in main offices, institutional goals and values will always push the life of the intellectual mind to the margins of main offices. School administrators wishing to champion a new instructional initiative must draw educational goals and values back into main office agendas and discussions. The degree to which a champion is granted access to managerial tools necessary to enact educational goals and values will be governed by two administrative assumptions. First, colleagues seated in main offices and in conference rooms must have confidence in the champion's ability to perform basic bureaucratic functions effectively and efficiently (see table 2.5). This confidence assures fellow administrators that the externalities of CCSM—rules, procedures, and practices—will be performed well.

Second, colleagues must have confidence that implementing the theories and practices of CCSM will not disrupt established institutional goals and organizational structures. This assures fellow school administrators that the champion will commit to doing the necessary homework to evaluate the school's organizational and instructional capacity to successfully adopt the goals and practices of CCSM (see table 2.8).

Although both assumptions appear to value managerial certainty over instructional ambiguity, administrators managing at the centers of main offices know that any effort to connect educational goals with administrative realities will set off a chain of organizational and instructional disruptions. With this unspoken assumption in mind, fellow school administrators trust that champions will apply the right mix of bureaucratic know-how and pedagogical knowledge to make these disruptions manageable.

When champions move between the margins and centers of main offices, there is a subtle shift in the lens through which other administrators and teachers see their jobs. School cultures change when a small group of people—champions—working in the margins of main offices, find a way for school communities to rely less on institutional realities and rely more on educational ideals.

Table 2.8 Champions Do Their Homework

CCSM COMPONENT	EVALUATION OF CCSM	Yes	No
Goal	Will CCSM help realize the goals in our school's mission statement?		
Theory	Can our staff make collective sense out of the theories that govern CCSM?		
Model	Do the goals and practices of CCSM align with our staff's content background and classroom experience?		
Systems	Will our school's instructional systems—mentoring, staff development, and curriculum development—be able to support the goals and practices of CCSM?		
Capacity	Will our school's organizational structure and resources be able to accommodate the goals and practices of CCSM?		
Strategy	Has our administrative team developed a comprehensive organizational and instructional strategy to enact the goals and practices of CCSM?		

RESOURCES

RESOURCE 2-1: Mission-Goal Alignment

Mission Statement Goals	CCSM Goals
Comprehensive preparation for college and career pathways	Make sense of problems and persevere in solving them
Knowledge, skills, and values required for productive global citizenship	Construct viable arguments
	Critique the reasoning of others
Highest educational standards	Use appropriate tools strategically
Meaningful learning experiences	Attend to precision
Critical thinking skills	Look for and make use of structure

RESOURCE 2-2: Instructional Narrative

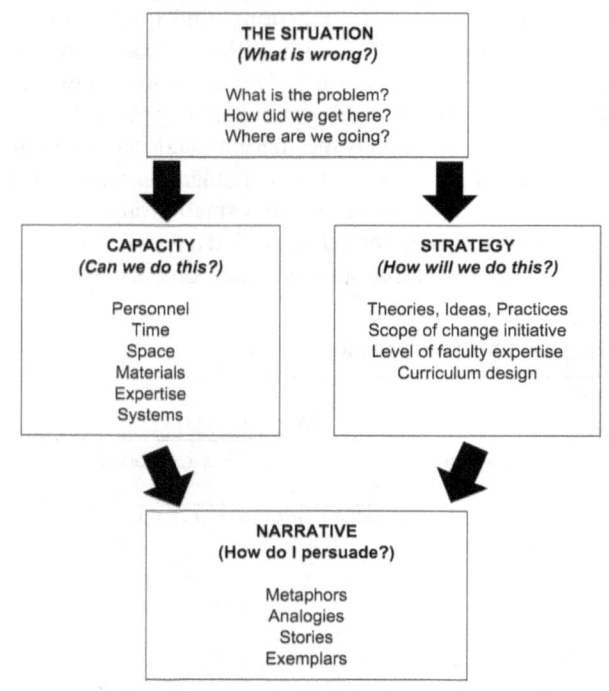

RESOURCE 2-3: Model Instructional Narrative: CCSM

Good Afternoon:

As you know, for the last three years the district has been in the process of adopting the common core standards for each subject in our curriculum. So far, the district has adopted standards for social studies, science, and language arts. This year, the district will adopt the common core standards in mathematics. Although I have expressed to you my reservations about the speed of these adoptions, I have no doubt that levels of thinking and methods of inquiry in these standards align perfectly with the educational goals and values in our school's mission statement. Of all the subjects addressed by the common core standards, I believe the mathematics standards offers a stark contrast between how we were all taught mathematics and what kinds of mathematical thinking our students need to acquire in the coming decade. Our decades-old practice of plug-and-chug math must give way to teaching strategies that provide our students with the ability to reason abstractly and quantitatively, to make sense out of problems, and to construct viable arguments and critique the reasoning of others.

Before I share with you the district's plan for adopting the new standards in mathematics, let me state to you my main concern about the new standards. The common core standards in mathematics requires an extensive academic background in mathematics. Most of us in this room, including myself, do not have a major or minor in mathematics—which, is a formidable obstacle to accurately teaching conceptual approaches to mathematical reasoning that the new math standards require.

Dr. Smith and his staff at the District Office acknowledged this concern and made the following changes to their original plan for adopting the new standards in mathematics:

First, unlike the other subject areas, the adoption of the math standards with be extended from a one-year adoption cycle to a three-year adoption cycle.

Second, the full adoption of math standards will be in the third year of the cycle. The first two years will allow faculty to learn and experiment with the theories, ideas, and practices of the new standards.

Third, the district will employ a full-time math coach. Her job will be to develop a curriculum and provide training sessions for our faculty.

Fourth, the district is committed to allocating sufficient monies to pay teachers for after-school and summer training.

Finally, and most importantly, the measurements of student progress on the standards will be solely a tool to provide teachers with the feedback they need to improve upon the teaching of the standards.

Later today and tomorrow, I will share with you the details of the training regime we have designed for implementing the new standards. Before we break, I want you to know that I am personally and professionally committed to the successful adoption of these standards. I have already informed my administrative staff that we will do whatever is necessary to support your efforts to learn and practice the new standards.

RESOURCE 2-4: Instructional Infrastructure

COMPONENT	FULLY ENACTED
Leadership	PURPOSE: Able to provide a coherent response to the five fundamental questions of schooling: LEARN, WORTH, ORGANIZE, ASSESS, TEACH. FRAME: Able to author a narrative that explains the relationship between an instructional problem, a theory-driven strategy for resolving the problem, and the organizational capacity to implement the strategy. CHALLENGE: Able to confront strongly held assumptions, beliefs, and practices about teaching and learning. INTEPRET: Able to apply theory-driven instructional initiatives to practical realities of the classroom: adopt, adapt, or discard. LEVERAGE: Able to enhance prior knowledge and skills. ALLOCATE: Able to position the appropriate resources (personnel, space, time, materials, expertise) in the right place at the right time. IMPLEMENT: Able to link goals (purpose + frame) with objectives (challenge + interpret + leverage + allocate) to achieve desired outcomes.
Instructional Systems	Are fully enacted: employment, mentoring, curriculum, teacher evaluation, and staff development Conform to goals and content of instructional worldview Help realize agreed-upon model of teaching
Administrative Commitment	Focuses on instruction Participates in training regime Deeply understands instructional worldview Adeptly conducts instructional conversations Regularly employs purposeful approaches to problem-solving Reinterprets state/district mandates
Organizational Commitment	Instructional initiatives align with worldview Resource allocation aligns with worldview and components of instructional culture Resource allocation is regularly adjusted Administrators become participants in implementing instructional initiatives Instructional time is protected Number and type of instructional initiatives are limited School routines are adopted to goals and content of instructional initiatives
Instructional Discourse	Honors diverse abilities, talents, and aspirations of student population Believes that parents will make best efforts to support the goals of schooling Demonstrates deep understandings of curriculum and instruction Demonstrates deep understandings of contemporary educational research Remains open to differing models of curriculum and instruction Holds deliberate meetings that are focused on teaching and learning Reflects on practice in a purposeful approach to problem-solving

RESOURCE 2-5: Training Regime

COMPONENT	WHAT TEACHERS ARE ASKED TO DO
Educate	Study content-based information on the theories, concepts, and practices of CCSM.
Model	Observe expert performance of theory-based methods.
Practice	Under the supervision of a mentor/consultant, apply theory-based methods in classroom.
Coach	Participate in ongoing conversations with mentor/consultant on gaps between the intentions of theory-based methods and actual performance of those methods in classrooms.
Practice	Under the supervision of a mentor/consultant, continue to employ feedback from coaching sessions to close gaps between intentions of theory-based methods and actual performance of those methods in classrooms.
Author	Construct pedagogical approaches and a plan of action that align with a school's instructional worldview, the social context of the school, and preexisting experiences.
Standardize	Normalize a set of teaching methods that make sense personally, are working, and accurately reflect the application of a theory-based method of instruction.

RESOURCE 2-6: Two Instructional Worldviews

FUNDAMENTAL QUESTIONS OF SCHOOLING	INSTRUCTIONAL WORLDVIEW A (To Prepare)	INSTRUCTIONAL WORLDVIEW B (To Educate)
What are the **GOALS** of schooling?	To prepare for an occupation To become proficient with a skill To follow directions	To pursue truth and rationality To become an analytical thinker and problem-solver To develop an authentic self
How do children **LEARN**?	Memorization Note-taking Worksheets	Inquiry Observation Practice Stories Discussions Projects
What knowledge is of most **WORTH**?	Facts Procedures Definitions	Big questions Big ideas Concepts
How should knowledge be **ORGANIZED**?	Units (in textbooks) Chapters (in textbooks) Course objectives Aligned with standards Breadth	Themes Interdisciplinary instruction Depth
How should we **ASSESS** what students understand?	Multiple choice testing Number right and wrong Grades Ranking	Performances/Projects/Exhibitions Demonstrated understandings of relationships between theories, ideas, concepts
How should we **TEACH**?	Set Objectives Present Information Model Check for Understanding Guided Practice Independent Practice	Facilitate Model Demonstrate Simulate Question Discuss
What **SKILLS** do we emphasize?	Associative Replicative Means, methods, routines, and techniques	Applicative Interpretative Ends, perspectives, models, and preferences
What should our students' **DISPOSITIONS** be?	Looking at what worked in the past Following directions Avoiding conflict Valuing systems and procedures over human judgment	Imagining Questioning assumptions Acknowledging complexity Seeing other perspectives Understanding limitations of knowledge Putting in proper context Remaining open-minded

RESOURCE 2-7: Agreed-Upon Model of Teaching

DOMAIN	DESCRIPTION
Purpose	The goal of each lesson is the solution to a messy or complex academic or societal problem.
Representation of the Discipline	Lesson reflects accurate representation of the discipline. Concepts are connected to subject matter facts and procedures.
High Cognitive Demand	Lessons include underlying concepts connected to subject matter procedures. Memorization of subject matter definitions, facts, and procedures always connects to academic concept or idea.
Students are Responsible for Thinking	Lessons and activities are designed to hold students responsible for resolving academic problems rather than relying on the teacher or textbook. Students are prompted to support solutions and claims with accepted authorities in the discipline.
Classroom Discourse	Advances beyond dominant teacher talk. Students frequently engage each other in purposeful discussions.
Lesson Sequence	Lesson is logical and accurately reflects disciplinary thinking.
Activity Structures	The arrangement of students, allocation of time, type of materials, degree of support, and form of technology all reflect the purpose and outcomes of the lesson.
Attention to Student Thinking	Teachers pay close attention what students say and do during a lesson so they can uncover and understand how they are thinking about theories, concepts, and practices in the discipline.
Lesson Outcomes	Students produce artifacts that reflect real-world applications and a deep understanding of disciplinary theories, concepts, and practices.
Lesson Coherence	There is alignment between purpose, discipline, cognitive demand, classroom discourse, activity structures, and lesson outcomes.

RESOURCE 2-8: Zone of Practicality

IS THE PROBLEM OR STRATEGY...	IMPLEMENTATION/ENACTMENT	YES	NO
Important?	Do teachers believe that this is a worthwhile problem or strategy to pursue?		
Concrete?	Are the adopted strategies composed of theories and practices that employ familiar vocabulary, concepts, and practices?		
Coherent?	Do the adopted strategies align with and leverage our school's instructional worldview?		
Teachable?	Do teachers possess the prior background knowledge to understand and practice the new strategy?		
Feasible?	Does the district/school possess the organizational resources—time, materials, space, and expertise—to train teachers and accommodate diverse instructional design features?		

RESOURCE 2-9: Implementing vs. Enacting

FUNCTION	IMPLEMENTATION Adopt→Adapt	ENACTMENT Replicate→Invent
Goals	Institutional	Educational
Time	Prescribed	Expansive
Space	Offices	Teacher Workplaces
Strategies	Routines	Ideas
Problems	Logistical	Relational
Change	Adopt→Adapt	Replicate→Invent
Performance	A Number	An Experience
Materials	Scripted	Authored
Vocabularies	Directive	Questioning

Chapter 3

Main Office C

> "Our number one goal for the coming school year is the successful implementation of our newly adopted student-first data management system."
>
> (Superintendent's Opening Day Address)

"I would like to thank you for your warm welcome. I am honored to join a district where excellence is a tradition. Our number one goal for the coming school year is the successful implementation of our student-first data management system. Later today, Larry McDonald, our new data management specialist, will describe all the capabilities of a system designed to keep parents informed, to hold students accountable, and to create a paperless school system."

THE FORMS OF SCHOOLING

No matter how skillful school administrators may be at championing the educational purposes of the offices they occupy, they will still return to main offices designed to achieve one or more of the forms of schooling listed below. None of the forms of schooling that fill administrative calendars support the educational goals of schooling—living up to a school's mission statement.

District Offices

District offices are dedicated to managing an image of schooling. The functions of central offices are aimed at creating an image of a district that is committed to some form of excellence: *"refuse to be ordinary," "a passion* for education," "new vision, new direction," "we can be the best," "a better school for a better tomorrow," "putting students first," "education is key," or "teamwork makes the dream work." Superintendents spend their days announcing and implementing new programs, new organizational structures, new buildings, and new technologies.

Building Offices

Building offices are dedicated to ordering the movement and progress of large groups of students. Principals spend their days scheduling and documenting the movement and academic progress of students.

Classrooms

Classrooms are dedicated to documenting the coverage of large amounts of subject matter content over short periods of time. Teachers spend their days carrying out instructional routines, enforcing classroom rules, and grading students.

While the design and function of each school workspace is different, they all support the same goal: managing a *form of schooling*. Whether managing an image, managing a system, or managing behavior, each office employs goals, plans, policies, procedures, rules, systems, standards, and routines to impose order and certainty on the organizational territories they control.

The managerial principle governing school organizations allows the forms of schooling to drive the functions of education. Superintendents, principals, and teachers enter their workspaces each day believing that informative newsletters, efficient systems, and quiet classrooms will activate the kinds of instruction that will achieve the educational goals and values listed in a district's mission statement. In reality, classrooms governed by managerial tools foster instructional regimes that, at best, constrain the pursuit of the goals listed in a school's mission statement and, at their worst, thwart any effort on the part of teachers to create classrooms that value differing learning styles, thoughtfulness, a sense of understanding, and compassion for others.

> *"I am concerned with the feedback I am receiving about our student-first data management system."*
>
> *(Superintendent to Principals)*

> *"Let me begin my apologizing for calling you out of your offices. I know this is a very busy time of the year. I felt it necessary to share with you my feedback about the adoption of the student-first data management system. I know the board has established the implementation of this program as a priority, but*

in reviewing the instructional programs you are currently working on, I see a large gap between how this accountability system works and what you have been working on in your classrooms."

THE FUNCTIONS OF EDUCATION

From an organizational standpoint, it is no surprise that school administrators feel more comfortable managing the forms of schooling than the functions of education. The job of school administration is made more certain and more secure when constructing master schedules, balancing budgets, allocating curricular materials, and implementing new technologies. The job of school administration becomes more uncertain when school administrators become involved in educational functions: addressing teacher performance, developing innovative instructional platforms, or tampering with the forms of schooling.

Even when educational functions are pushed into a schoolwide conversation, school administrators transform the educational question into a managerial form of schooling: a number, a facility, a cost, a technology, or an activity. Table 3.1 illustrates how educational goals expressed in District 93's mission statement (see Resource 3-1) are translated into managerial forms of governance: to *adopt*, to *develop*, to *add*, to *approve*, to *employ*, and to *expand*. The goals, strategies, methods, and language of managerial tools are not designed to educate, to facilitate, or to coach. They are designed to implement the managerial functions of telling, allocating, and inspecting.

Table 3.1 When Functions of Education Become Forms of Schooling

FUNCTIONS OF EDUCATION (District 93's Mission Statement)		FORMS OF SCHOOLING
"A challenging learning environment"	becomes	ADOPTION of standards
"High expectations for success"	becomes	DEVELOPMENT of a new grading policy
"Development-appropriate instruction"	becomes	ADDITION of a 24/7 online tutoring program
"Establishes values to act with thoughtfulness and sense of understanding and compassion for others"	becomes	APPROVAL of character education program
"Student's self-esteem is fostered by positive relationships with students and staff"	becomes	EMPLOYMENT of additional social worker
"Strive to have parents, teachers, and community members actively involved in our students' learning"	becomes	EXPANSION of parent advisory council

With the forms of schooling in firm control of the functions of education, the following educational questions are never asked at school board meetings:

Board Member	*"Dr. Lewis, could you describe how the goal of critical thinking in your strategic plan will be taught in our schools?"*
Parent	*"Dr. Lewis, how are the worksheets my son is completing for homework meeting the goal of high cognitive demand?"*
Board Member	*"Dr. Lewis, how are the opportunities to learn listed in our mission statement addressing the gender gap in our upper-level science courses?"*
Parent	*"Dr. Lewis, would you describe how teachers would use iPads to teach the five habits of thought outlined in your September Newsletter?"*
Board Member	*"Dr. Lewis, please explain how adaptive reasoning listed in the district's mission statement is being taught in our schools."*
Parent	*"Dr. Lewis, please explain how our new science facility will develop the innovative mind that you reference in your newsletter."*
Board Member	*"Dr. Lewis, do you see a contradiction between standards-based curriculum and your goal of expanding elective course offerings?"*
Parent	*"Dr. Lewis, why must every student go to college?"*

Asking educational questions is rarely, if ever, pursued by members of the school community. Board members and parents lack the educational backgrounds to question how a form of schooling—the number of computers in school—would result in an educational outcome of schooling—critical thinking. Educational discussions arise when administrators attempt to employ managerial responses to a parent questioning why their son or daughter is showing an indifference to schooling. Citing a number, a technology, a program, or a technique tells parents little, if anything, about why the interactions between teachers, students, and tasks are failing to resonate with their son or daughter.

A well-thought-out educational explanation connects the *why* of schooling, with the *what* and the *how* of schooling. Figure 3.1 illustrates the process that school administrators would employ to connect educational values expressed in school mission statements to the daily functions of classrooms. Aligning

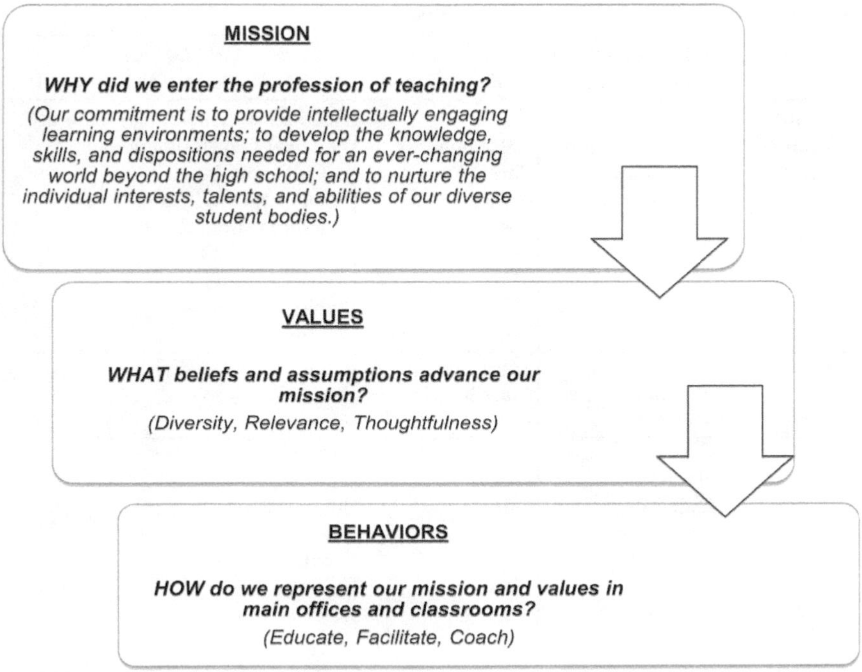

MISSION

WHY did we enter the profession of teaching?

(Our commitment is to provide intellectually engaging learning environments; to develop the knowledge, skills, and dispositions needed for an ever-changing world beyond the high school; and to nurture the individual interests, talents, and abilities of our diverse student bodies.)

VALUES

WHAT beliefs and assumptions advance our mission?

(Diversity, Relevance, Thoughtfulness)

BEHAVIORS

HOW do we represent our mission and values in main offices and classrooms?

(Educate, Facilitate, Coach)

Figure 3.1 Connecting the Why, What, and How of Schooling.

educational values with classroom realities reorients the proper placement of the forms and functions of schooling. Managers permit the forms of schooling to control the functions of education. Educators place the functions of teaching and learning in control of the managerial forms of schooling (see Resource 3-2).

MAIN OFFICE A AND B

Standing in the way of connecting the *why, what,* and *how* of schooling—living up to a school's mission statement—are main offices and classrooms structured around systems and routines designed to efficiently implement the forms of schooling. The dominant role bureaucratic and professional functions assume in school organizations will translate any effort to live up to a school's mission statement into a managerial function. With this organizational reality in mind, how does a school administrator reassert the role that educational functions should be playing in schools?

Table 3.2 What Main Office Are You Sitting In?

	MAIN OFFICE A (Managerial)	MAIN OFFICE B (Professional)	MAIN OFFICE C (Educational)
Aims and Goals of Schooling	Measurement Documentation Compliance Efficiency Funding	Track Credential Rank Award Prepare	Academic (Cultivating Humanity) Personal Development (Self-Cultivation) Socialization (Citizenship & Interpersonal Relations) Economic Productivity (Vocational) Lifelong Learning (Reflective Thinking)
Functions	Tell Allocate Inspect	Train Classify Assess	Educate Facilitate Coach
Tools	Goals Plans Policies Procedures Rules Systems	Specialists Programs Guides Surveys Data Professional Development	Listening Studying Interpreting Designing Modeling Piloting Redesigning

Table 3.2 compares the goals, functions, and tools used by managerial, professional, and educational administrators. Administrators with different orientations will employ different sets of organizational and instructional tools to pursue their goals. Managers are most comfortable working with the organizational tools housed in Main Offices A and B. Educators are most comfortable working with the instructional tools housed in Main Office C. The mindsets of those seated in main offices determine the set of tools used on a daily basis.

School administrators in Main Offices A & B approach the initiatives piled in their in-boxes as a managerial problem: how to efficiently reduce the pile of initiatives. The most efficient strategy for moving paper out of main office in-boxes is to tell, allocate, and inspect (see figure 3.2). These managerial functions work so well in Main Offices A & B due to organizational tools that

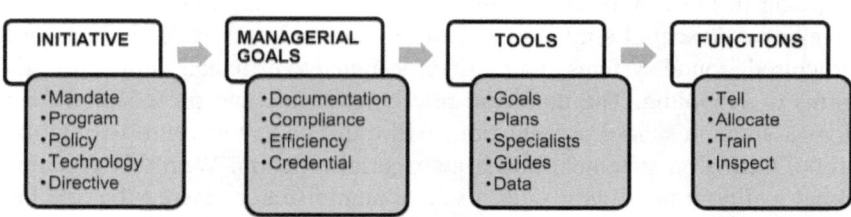

Figure 3.2 Moving Paper Out of In-Boxes in Main Office A and B.

provide school administrators with public ways of showing compliance—test scores, curriculum handbooks, and certifications—without disrupting comfortable organizational and instructional routines.

On the first day of school, teachers in classrooms surrounding Main Offices A and B will be issued a box of curriculum materials, a schedule of in-service sessions, and the accountability forms they will be required to complete. Along with these boxes, schedules, and forms, a consultant will present a fifty-minute PowerPoint presentation on the goals and content of the initiative. The last five PowerPoint slides show how the forms they received in the loose-leaf binders should be completed.

GETTING TO MAIN OFFICE C

Administrators in Main Office C enter their offices with a very different managerial and instructional mindset than their colleagues in Main Offices A and B. Central to this mindset is understanding the relationship between the *aims, forms, and functions* of the schools they lead. The *aims* of schooling are those educational goals and values listed in school mission statements—what schools ought to be doing. The *forms* of schooling are the institutional and professional goals listed in mandates, policy manuals, rules and regulations, and programs—what outside interests expect schools to do. The *functions* of schooling are what administrators and teachers actually do in their offices and classrooms on a daily basis. Administrators in Main Office C see their roles in the main office as translating educational aims into daily instructional functions; guarding against the colonization of instructional functions by institutional and professional forms of schooling; and maintaining a public image of the forms of schooling.

THE DILEMMA OF MAIN OFFICE C

School administrators will find themselves in a dilemma when mandated to implement a method of teaching that is in direct opposition to methods designed to live up to mission statement goals. Too often, mandated initiatives align well with institutional forms of schooling, but fail to address educational aims.

Administrators in Main Office C resolve this dilemma by employing a mix of managerial and educational tools to enact the rules, policies, mandates, directives, and programs that land in their in-boxes at the beginning of the school year. Figure 3.3 illustrates the educational and institutional

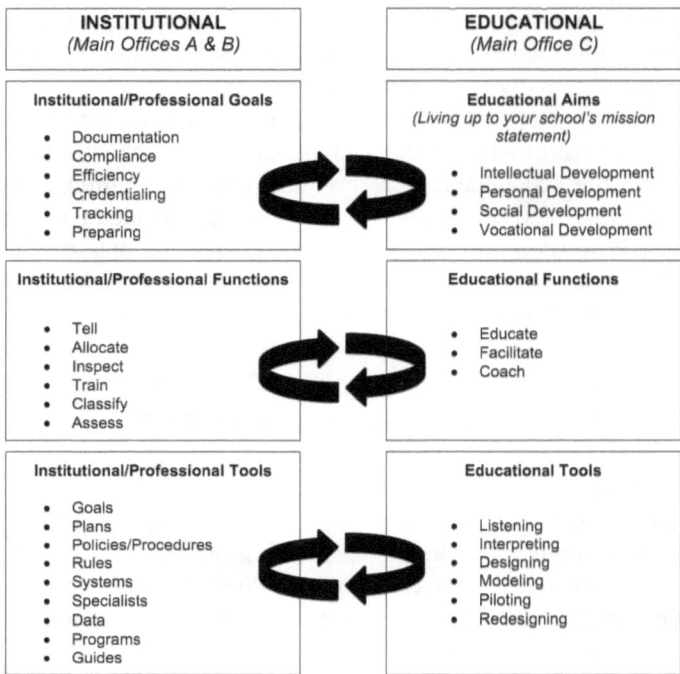

Figure 3.3 Blending Mindsets to Implement Initiatives.

mindsets that await every new instructional initiative entering a main office. Administrators in Main Office C spend their days crafting strategies that blend the goals, functions, and tools lodged in Main Office A, B, and C in ways that both achieve the full implementation of an educational aim, while at the same time, leave the forms of schooling untouched by the educational aim.

In the case of common core standards, administrators in Main Office C would devote considerable time, resources, and expertise to reproduce the models of teaching that promote the levels of thinking and methods of inquiry represented in the common core standards. At the same time, administrators in Main Office C would pay close attention to the managerial tasks of complying with accountability mandates and protecting the normal routines of schooling from any potential disruptions caused by implementing common core.

The same strategy would be employed when an initiative is clearly an institutional goal. Most state-mandated standardized testing programs would fall into this category. School administrators in Main Office C would lean toward the institutional functions and tools necessary for complying with the mandate and, at the same time, protect the classroom from accountability measures that would disrupt the enactment of common core.

Strong accountability mandates might also contain opportunities to transform an institutional form of schooling into an educational function. Newer versions of state testing programs and the ACT/SAT are now requiring the kinds of thinking and communicating that are embodied in common core. Administrators in Main Office C would view these newer versions of the state testing program as an opportunity to leverage newly adopted teaching models to help realize an educational aim.

Even with a solid history of decision-making that favors the functions over the forms of a new instructional initiative, administrators in Main Office C will continually be drawn into a process of making collective sense out of the contradictory goals, functions, and tools of main offices A, B, and C. Without a well-thought-out response to the educational and organizational worldviews that control main offices (see Resource 3-3), administrators in Main Office C will see the goals and methods of a new instructional initiative become institutionalized in Main Office A or muddled in Main Office B.

Each worldview poses questions that form the foundation of a school culture: Why are we here? How do we talk about why we are here? How do we practice why we are here? A well-thought-out response to the questions posed by each worldview creates a compelling reason for teachers to believe, to judge, and to act. Only when a school administration and teachers agree on the *why* of schooling will they be ready to live up to the educational aims of school mission statements.

RESOURCES

RESOURCE 3-1: District 93 Mission Statement

District 93 seeks to create a challenging learning environment that encourages high expectations for success through developmentally appropriate instruction that allows for individual differences and learning styles. Our school establishes values to act with thoughtfulness and a sense of understanding and compassion for others. Each student's self-esteem is fostered by positive relationships with students and staff. We strive to have our parents, teachers, and community members actively involved on our students' learning.

RESOURCE 3-2: Forms and Functions

OFFICE	MANAGING (Forms drive Functions)			LEADING (Functions drive Forms)	
	FORMS OF SCHOOLING	→	FUNCTIONS OF EDUCATION	FUNCTIONS OF EDUCATION	→ FORMS OF SCHOOLING
Central Office	• Boilers • Budgets • Boosters		• Marketing • Adopting • Networking	• Vision • Instructional systems • Administrative structure • Allocation of resources • Instructional discourse • Social arrangements of instruction	• Mission statement • Employment • Curriculum development • Performance evaluation • Staff development
Main Office	• Courses • Credits • Schedules		• Organizing • Inspecting • Documenting	• Master schedule • Curriculum development • Teacher evaluation • Induction • Training	• Electives • Teacher assignments • Textbook adoption • Curriculum proposals • Evaluation cycles • Mentoring • Coaching
Classroom	• Rules • Assignments • Grades		• Telling • Enforcing • Evaluating	• Norms of teaching (how) • Theories (what and why) • Strategies (how, what, and why)	• Replicate\Interpret • Lecture\Facilitate • Memorize\Discover • Facts\Concepts • Tests\Performance • Right answers\right questions

RESOURCE 3-3: Worldviews

WORLDVIEW	FUNDAMENTAL QUESTIONS
Educational Worldview	What is this school about? What is important here? What do we believe in? Why do we function the way we do? How are we unique?
Instructional Worldview	What are the goals of schooling? How do children learn? What skills do we emphasize? What should our students' dispositions be? What knowledge is of most worth? How should knowledge be organized? How should we assess what students understand? How should we teach?
Pedagogical Worldview	What beliefs, theories, and practices govern a new instructional initiative? What gaps exist between the beliefs, theories, and practices of a new instructional initiative and the beliefs, theories, and practices of the classrooms in my school? What organizational and instructional strategies should I pursue to close the gap between the goals and practices of a new instructional initiative and the goals and practices of the classrooms in my school?
Organizational Worldview	What knowledge of contemporary trends in teaching and learning should administrators possess to successfully implement a new instructional initiative? What knowledge and skills must faculty possess to successfully implement a new instructional initiative? What organizational and material capacities must a district have in place to support sophisticated staff development programs? What theories and practices of a new instructional initiative align with the district's educational aims and instructional worldview? What beliefs, ideas, and vocabularies represent a shared commitment to the educational goals and values written into school mission statements? What is the community's level of support for innovative approaches to teaching and learning?

Chapter 4

Silver Bullets

> *"Dr. Smith has authorized me to bring in Dr. Lorrie Crowley, a Reading First consultant. At our next team meeting, Dr. Crowley will outline the goals of the program and a schedule for program adoption."*
>
> *(Memorandum to Principals from Assistant Superintendent)*

COMMUNITY HIGH SCHOOL DISTRICT 108

<u>MEMORANDUM</u>

To: F. Jones, A. Johnson, G. Lowman, C. Singleton

From: T. Jenkins, Assistant Superintendent for Curriculum and Instruction

Subject: "Reading First"

As you know, the board has expressed concern about our declining tests scores in reading. Dr. Smith has authorized me to bring in Dr. Lorrie Crowley, a Reading First consultant. At our next team meeting, Dr. Crowley will outline the goals of the program and a schedule for program adoption.

At this same meeting, we will discuss the anti-bullying program we initiated last year.

Each of us in the Central Office would like to thank all building personnel for embracing the Dare program. Police Chief Lawnson has called me several times about how well the program is going.

TELLING, SELLING, INSTALLING

In the process of restructuring and repurposing schools, the everyday managerial tools that school administrators employ to implement a school program, or to address emerging organizational and instructional problems, go largely unrecognized. While all of these managerial tools fit well within main offices that pursue institutional goals and functions, they serve as obstacles to administrators seeking to live up to their schools' mission statements.

One of the most common managerial tools entering main offices each year are *Silver Bullet* packages that market fast solutions to whatever organizational or instructional problem a school may be encountering. The managerial attributes that make Silver Bullet programs so appealing to school administrators are as follows:

Simplicity over Complexity

Silver bullets reduce the messy process of interpreting and applying theory-based instructional initiatives into a simple managerial process of telling, selling, and installing the already-defined goals and practices of the program (see figure 4.1). School managers are much more comfortable with administering the managerial artifacts of a silver bullet solution than supervising the subjective understandings of the beliefs and practices of a silver bullet solution.

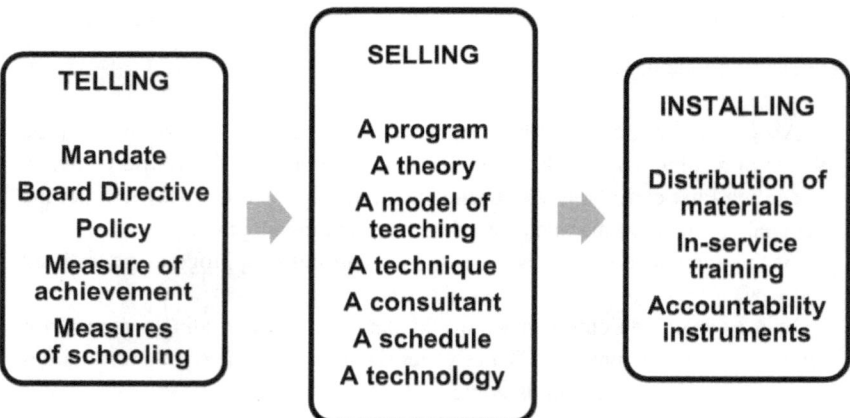

Figure 4.1   Loading Silver Bullets.

Accountability over Responsibility

Silver bullet solutions remove administrative responsibility for producing advertised outcomes. The highly prescriptive components of silver bullet solutions—goals, theories, protocols, assessments, and materials—hold school administrators responsible only for managing the inputs of the program and documenting the outputs of the program. The responsibility for producing the advertised *educational outcomes* of the program rest solely with the program, students, teachers, and parents.

Adaptation over Adoption

Rather than *adopt* a new initiative in its entirety, school administrators will *adapt* a silver bullet solution. Administrators will implement any theories, ideas, or practices of the silver bullet solution that can be easily added to existing rules, procedures, and systems. Those components of the program that cannot be easily added are adapted to fit established organizational norms or discarded.

Certainty over Uncertainty

Silver bullet solutions are designed to replace established organizational and instructional routines with new beliefs, theories, and practices. Managerial mindsets do not share the same enthusiasm for any theory, program, technology, or technique that threatens the workings of established organizational and instructional routines. Yes, accepted organizational or instructional routines may not be working well, but they are working. Why disrupt a school routine that is not broken?

While the attributes of Silver Bullet programs are attractive to managerial mindsets, they foster attitudes that impair any effort to reproduce the theories, ideas, and practices promoted by the program. Teachers' experiences with managerial-driven Silver Bullet programs lead to a *this too shall pass* attitude toward the announcement of programs designed to check off implementing surface features of a program. Administrators' experiences with managerial-driven Silver Bullet programs lead to a *we've tried this before* attitude toward the announcement of programs lacking the organizational and professional development infrastructure to fully implement program theories, ideas, and practices.

Both attitudes are in full display each school year with administrators and teachers participating in a ritual dance around the theories, ideas, and practices of newly announced Silver Bullet programs. Teachers unpack boxes. Administrators distribute forms. Students fill in bubble sheets.

"In reading this study I was struck by the amount of time we are allocating for reading and our inability to schedule common planning times for staff development. It appears that we have implemented a number of programs in the last three years that have reduced the time allocated for reading and the scheduling flexibility we would need to accommodate teacher training."

(Superintendent to Principals)

COMMUNITY HIGH SCHOOL DISTRICT 108

MEMORANDUM

To: F. Jones, A. Johnson, G. Lowman, C. Singleton

From: T. Jenkins, Assistant Superintendent for Curriculum and Instruction

Subject: "Reading Study"

As you know, the board has expressed a concern about our declining tests scores in reading. This summer, members of the reading team met with Dr. Lorrie Crowley, a reading specialist from Lincoln University, to examine our school's reading program. This afternoon, Dr. Crowley and Lorrie Thomson, our reading team leader, will share with you the results of the study and the committee's plan for strengthening our current program.

In reading the study I was struck by the amount of time we are allocating for reading and our inability to schedule common planning times for staff development. It appears that we have implemented a number of programs in the last three years that have reduced the time allocated for reading and the scheduling flexibility we would need to accommodate teacher training. I will study this issue further, but we may have reached the point where we prioritize the instructional goals we want to pursue and construct schedules reflecting those priorities. This may mean discarding or scaling back on established programs in our buildings.

ASSESSING AND FACILITATING

Silver Bullet programs expose school administrators to theories, concepts, and practices gaining currency in the educational marketplace of ideas. In this shallow exposure, managerial mindsets ignore the relationships between the *what* and *why* of the program—goals and theories—and the *how* of the program—activity structures, content organization, teaching roles, student roles, and assessment protocols.

Without attention to the educative function of a silver bullet program—the *what* and *why*—the *how* of the program becomes a confused mix of surface representations of the program, slightly modified teaching patterns and misconstrued teaching methodologies. The resulting muddle over the ends and means of a Silver Bullet programs triggers the annual ritual of adapting and then discarding the Silver Bullet programs of the day.

If properly aimed, Silver Bullet programs are powerful vehicles for living up to school mission statements. School administrators taking aim with a Silver Bullet programs must ask a series of questions to determine the worth and practicality of the program's theories and practices. Affirmative answers to the questions listed below indicate that the program contains all the elements of an effective organizational strategy: agrees with an organizational vision (coherence), helps realize an organizational vision (continuity), and implements an organizational vision (feasibility).

Query #1: Do the program's theories and practices align with a school's agreed-upon instructional worldview (see Resource 4-1)?

Query #2: Will the program's theories and practices help realize an agreed-upon educational goal?

Query #3: Do the program's theories and practices align with an agreed-upon model of teaching (see Resource 4-2)?

Query #4: Are the program's theories and practices open to modification?

Query #5: Does the district or school have the capacity to implement the program and its theories and practices (see Resource 4-3)?

The final outcome of the aiming process is the decision by a school administrator to "pull the trigger" on the program or elements of the program. At this point, the administrator either decides to adopt the entire program, adapt parts of the program, or to discard the entire program. Table 4.1 shows how one school staff might respond to various present-day Silver Bullet programs.

In determining the worth and practicality of the *Reading Recovery* program, for example, the staff decided to fully *adopt* the theories, practices, and structure of the program. School staff had determined that the pedagogical model represented in the program was consistent with how teachers believe reading should be taught and it would augment what teachers were already practicing in classrooms. Even though the Reading Recovery program leaves little to no room for program modification (Query #4), school staff decided to value program coherence over program experimentation.

Table 4.1 Adopt, Adapt, or Discard

SILVERBULLETPROGRAM	QUERY#1	QUERY#2	QUERY#3	QUERY#4	QUERY#5	ACTION
Reading Recovery	Yes	Yes	Yes	No	Yes	*Adopt*
Common Core Standards	Yes	Yes	Yes	Yes	Yes	*Adapt*
Assertive Discipline	No	No	No	No	Yes	*Discard*
Conceptual Mathematics	Yes	Yes	Yes	Yes	Yes	*Adapt*
Reading First	No	No	No	No	Yes	*Discard*
Saxon Mathematics	No	No	No	No	Yes	*Discard*
Learning Communities	Yes	Yes	Yes	Yes	Yes	*Adapt*
Character Counts	No	No	No	No	Yes	*Discard*
Interdisciplinary Courses	Yes	Yes	Yes	Yes	Yes	*Adapt*

In determining the worth and practicality of Assertive Discipline, a Silver Bullet behavior management program, school staff decided that it was in opposition to their beliefs about how children learn and how children should be treated. In this case, they decided to *discard* the Silver Bullet program.

Silver Bullet programs are here to stay in schools. Packages of theories, practices, and solutions offer busy school administrators' vehicles for bringing into their schools what is considered to be best practices in the field of education. Silver bullet programs do offer schools theories, ideas, and practices having the potential to improve the quality of schooling experienced by administrators, teachers, and students.

At the same time, however, the adoption of a Silver Bullet program could disrupt the momentum of programs already in place. Changing organizational and instructional beliefs and practices is a cumulative process of mastering a series of routines and techniques that over time will accurately reflect the goals and methods of a new pedagogical model. The annual introduction of a new Silver Bullet program promotes a new body of theories and practices that can disrupt the mastery process. Without program continuity, teachers will be reluctant to commit to replacing comfortable teaching routines with ever-changing theories, ideas, and practices.

PULLING THE TRIGGER

Managerial mindsets never wrestle with questions of program worth, continuity, or coherence. When handed a Silver Bullet program by the state or central office, school managers load and fire. In the busy process of telling, allocating, and inspecting, managerial administrators never consider whether the program hits the educational target. Educational mindsets always look at educational goals first—the *what* and *why*—before proceeding to the *how* of program implementation. Educators pull no organizational triggers until they are certain that a goal is worth hitting and that the instructional and behavioral models of the program are worth practicing.

RESOURCES

RESOURCE 4-1: Instructional Worldview

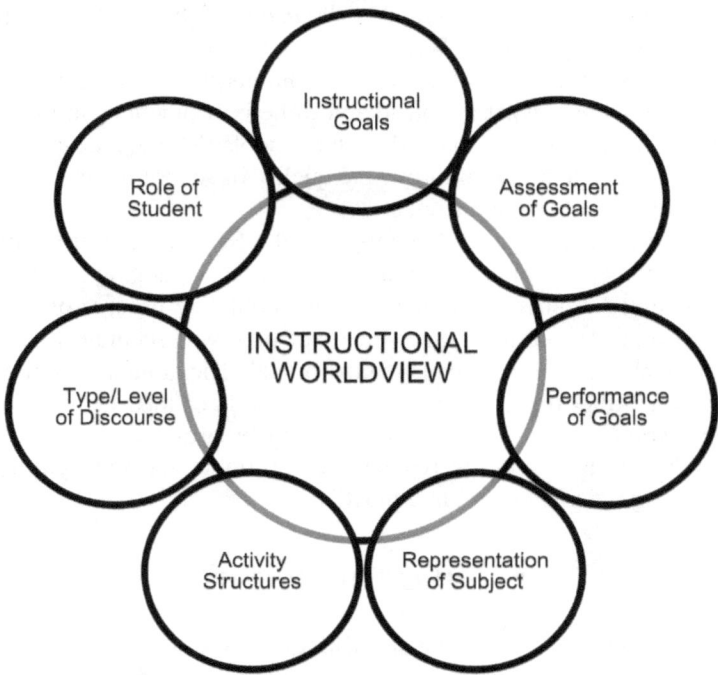

RESOURCE 4-2: How We Teach

Learning Environments	Attention to unique educational styles Acknowledgment of multiple sources of education Valuing the multiple aims/functions of schooling Evidence of high student engagement with subject matter, teacher, and other students Multiple activity structures taking place simultaneously
Pedagogical Methods	Cases/Scenarios/Stories Problem-based Personal modeling (living exemplars of certain virtues or attitudes) Discussion Argumentation
Curricular Content	Thematic Interdisciplinary Problem-based Functional

RESOURCE 4-3: Organizational Capacity

HUMAN AND ORGANIZATIONAL RESOURCES	SHARED NORMS AND EXPECTATIONS
Level of Professionalism	Involvement in professional organizations Involvement in school-level professional development Involvement in school improvement committees Knowledge of contemporary trends in teaching and learning
Level of Community Support	Satisfied with curriculum offerings Satisfied with teaching methodologies Satisfied with safety of building Willing to grant administrators and faculty autonomy
Level of Complexity	New initiatives align with knowledge and skill levels of faculty District organizational and material capacities support appropriate staff development programs Teachers are given the appropriate time, space, materials, and expertise to learn new pedagogies
Level of Implementation	Newly adopted programs are coherent, continuous, and pursue a valued end of schooling Organizational systems support new theories, ideas, and practices District establishes realistic timelines for implementation
Level of Resources	District provides appropriate time, materials, space, and expertise for staff development District commits to providing resources over extended periods of time
Level of Culture	Faculty share a commitment to the educational goals and values written into school mission statement Faculty share a commitment to school's instructional worldview Faculty share a commitment to school's embedded staff development activities School discourse (vocabularies) reflect positive attitudes toward students and parents and high expectations for teaching and learning Interactions between staff evidence a spirit of friendship and community The atmosphere of the school embraces change and continuous improvement

Chapter 5

Following Through

> *At our first administrative council meeting, please bring with you the completed "Setting Goals" template. Dr. Anna McCarthy, our program consultant, will review the completed goals template and review the steps for implementing stage two of the program.*
>
> *(Superintendent to Principals)*

COMMUNITY HIGH SCHOOL DISTRICT 108

<u>MEMORANDUM</u>

To: All Principals

From: C. Franklyn, Superintendent

Subject: Common Core Standards

The Board is excited about the adoption of Common Core Standards. At our opening day institute, all principals received an in-service session on program implementation, a box of materials for distribution to teachers, and five program templates to document the completion of each stage of program implementation. At our first administrative council meeting, please bring with you the completed "Setting Goals" template. Dr. Anna McCarthy, our program consultant, will review the completed goals template and review the steps for implementing stage two of the program.

Table 5.1 Following Up

TASK	ROUTINED
Establish GOALS	What tasks and functions are measurable?
Establish TASKS	How should tasks and functions be sequenced?
Establish RULES	What policies and procedures are required to implement tasks and functions?
Establish SCHEDULE	How should tasks and functions be scheduled?
Establish BUDGET	How should we allocate resources?
Inspect	How will we document program outcomes?

FOLLOWING UP

Most managerial conversations in main offices end with one administrator asking another administrator to *follow up* on some course of action. Whatever terminology an administrator chooses to use—touch base, get back to me, or keep me in the loop—gathering feedback on the progress of a course of action is considered an essential managerial function. All administrators learn early on in their careers that without timely and accurate feedback, they leave themselves open to the original sin of school administration: being blindsided.

Managerial mindsets narrowly define the feedback function as checking off a series of discrete tasks that document the implementation of a new instructional initiative or organizational arrangement: announcing the program, establishing a budget, distributing materials, employing a consultant, scheduling training sessions, and collecting progress reports. If timelines are met, materials are accounted for, and the appropriate checklists are handed in, managerial mindsets are satisfied that the follow-up function has been fully performed.

Table 5.1 list a set of managerial routines that school administrators would employ in performing the follow-up function. Each managerial move concentrates on the performance, measurement, organization, cost, and documentation of the external components of a program, mandate, or policy. Managerial mindsets believe the efficient implementation of the forms of a program—distributing materials, scheduling workshops, or employing a consultant—translates into the full implementation of the substance of the program.

> *Please note that our quarterly administrative meetings will be devoted to examining hard and soft data on the progress of this initiative. At each of these meetings, we will develop strategies for addressing problems with the program and establish benchmarks for project completion.*
>
> *(Superintendent to Principals)*

COMMUNITY HIGH SCHOOL DISTRICT 108

MEMORANDUM

To: All Principals

From: C. Franklyn, Superintendent

Subject: Common Core Standards

The Board is pleased with the progress we have made on the adoption of Common Core Standards. In our summer study groups with Dr. Anna McCarthy, we further refined the curriculum templates we will use to expand the writing project into the remaining subject areas. Attached is a schedule listing the time and dates Dr. McCarthy will be in your building to observe classrooms and sit with teachers in their LC's to gather feedback on progress with the new curriculum. Please note that our quarterly administrative meetings will be devoted to examining hard and soft data on the progress of this initiative. At each of these meetings, we will develop strategies for addressing problems with the program and establish benchmarks for project completion. Dr. McCarthy and I will lead these meetings.

FOLLOWING THROUGH

Educational mindsets view the feedback function as an essential component of an educational process designed to make collective sense out of the practical applications of a new instructional initiative: evaluating staff readiness, teaching new theories and practices, interpreting new theories and practices, applying new theories and practices, organizing for new theories and practices, and modifying new theories and practices. *Following through* is not an event or a task or a function. Following through draws administrators and teachers into a learning cycle that offers staff the opportunity to add to their skill set or enhance the skills they have already mastered.

Table 5.2 outlines a set of educational functions that school administrators would employ to assist faculty with making collective sense out of the *what, why,* and *how* of a new school improvement initiative. Educational mindsets assume responsibility for both components of the feedback task: *following up* on the implementation of a new school improvement initiative, and *following through* on the mastery of new beliefs, theories, and practices in the classroom.

Table 5.2 Following Through

TASKS	LEARNING CYCLE
Listening	What does the faculty believe about teaching and learning?
Educating	How does this initiative connect with what we are doing already?
Interpreting	What will work/not work for our school?
Coaching	How do we practice this initiative?
Facilitating	How will the organization accommodate this new instructional initiative?
Redesigning	How do we adjust the learning cycle to accommodate gaps in understanding and performance?

THE DECISION TO FOLLOW THROUGH

When a new school improvement initiative lands in main office in-boxes, most school administrators choose to *follow up* on the implementation of the initiative. The managerial tasks involved in following up—checking boxes, conducting inventories, and handing in forms—prevents administrators from becoming drawn into a complex process of educating, facilitating, and coaching. Before making the decision to *follow up* or *follow through* on a school improvement initiative, school administrators should be fully aware of the following managerial-leadership tradeoffs that will be present in any change initiative.

Following through Will Cause Conflict

Any alteration in teaching methodology will prompt feelings of inadequacy and insecurity. No matter how well-thought-out or resourced a new instructional initiative maybe, asking teachers to step out of their pedagogical comfort zone will be met with varying degrees of resistance. The decision to *follow up* leaves administrators alone to collect checklists and teachers alone to fill out checklists. The decision to *follow through* will involve a long and patient educative process that builds trust, enthusiasm, and competence among a skeptical faculty.

Following through Will Require Doing Your Homework

Most of today's school improvement initiatives ask school administrators to put in place training regimes and organizational structures that redefine accepted teaching methodologies. Unlike school improvement initiatives that add a technique or a technology to an existing practice, today's research-driven initiatives ask teachers to reconstruct how they think about the teaching of subject matter content.

The complex process of translating theory into everyday classroom practice must be guided by school administrators who fully understand the theories and practices they are endorsing. Without understanding the *why* of a new instructional initiative, school administrators will be unable to take an active role in developing the organizational goals and arrangements that support the deep learning of a new pedagogical model.

Understanding the *why* of a program, a teaching model, or a curriculum design, draws a school administrator into a personal journey of reading, studying, questioning, and ultimately modeling the beliefs, values, and principles of a new school improvement initiative—they do their homework. Without the *"why,"* the *how* and *what* of a school improvement initiative will be reduced to surface representations or misrepresentations of ambitious models of teaching and learning.

Following through Requires the Redesign of Organizational and Instructional Systems

Managerial mindsets consider the one-day workshop, the curriculum binder, and an ASCD video as an adequate commitment to understanding and practicing a new instructional initiative. The decision to *follow up* is reduced to the delivery of materials, the recording of attendance at a workshop, and the completion of a form.

The decision to *follow through* on an instructional initiative commits school administrators to the following managerial and educative functions:

- Organizing large blocks of time for learning and practicing.
- Purchasing materials that are customized for particular school circumstances.
- Employing consultants that have the time and venues to observe, model, and coach teachers.
- Redesigning organizational routines to fit the goals, beliefs, and practices of a new pedagogical model.

Following through Redefines the Ends and Means of Implementation

Managerial mindsets define the process of implementation as the completion and documentation of discrete managerial tasks: materials distributed, consultants employed, workshops scheduled, rooms assigned, schedules developed, forms collected, and reports sent to central offices. All functions in the implementation process are instrumental. The only distinction between the ends and means of *following up* is *when* a managerial task is performed. The allocation and scheduling function occur at the beginning of the implementation process; the collection and documentation function occur at the end of the implementation process.

School administrators who decide to *follow through* on an instructional initiative view the end and means of implementation as an educative process. The *end* of *following through* is the enactment of educational values and goals in daily classroom instruction—living up to a school's mission statement. The *means* of *following through* is leading and participating in a continuous learning process that connects educational values and goals to daily classroom practices.

Following through Calls into Question Accepted Beliefs, Values, and Practices

During the feedback process of *following through*, a school administrator may discover that deeply held beliefs about teaching and learning are mistaken. The decision to *follow up* avoids challenges to educational beliefs and values by concentrating solely on the proper execution of managerial tasks: telling, allocating, and inspecting. The decision to *follow through* immerses school administrators in an educational process that not only questions the substance of an instructional initiative but also asks administrators and teachers to expand upon their understandings of concepts, theories, and practices in curriculum, instruction, and school organization.

Whatever theories, ideas, or practices become the focus of *following through*, a true educative process will at some point throw into question the usefulness of a well-regarded instructional practice or school routine.

FOLLOWING UP OR FOLLOWING THROUGH ON COMMON CORE

What follows is a description of how two administrative mindsets would interpret and enact the feedback function when charged with implementing the common core standards.

FOLLOWING UP on Common Core

Managerial mindsets begin the process of *following up* on common core with the assumption that this instructional initiative, like all other mandated reforms, is this year's add-on program to be installed in classrooms. After the opening day presentation of telling staff the *why* of the mandate (the state told us to do it), the *what* of the mandate (found in loose leaf binders), and the *how* of the mandate (scheduled half-day workshops), managerial mindsets fill their calendars with the tasks of *following up*: they tell teachers what to do, they tell teachers when to do it, they distribute materials, they organize workshops, they review lesson plans, they conduct random observations, they administer quarterly assessments, and they report on what they have distributed, attended, and observed.

Teachers spend the subsequent months responding to *follow-up* tasks: they unpack boxes, they attend workshops, they write lesson plans, they perform surface representations of common core standards, they allocate time for prepping their students for the quarterly assessment, and they complete the appropriate forms documenting their compliance with the common core initiative.

If students perform poorly on the state assessment of common core knowledge and skills, administrators will spend the summer adding, subtracting, or modifying *follow-up* tasks: purchasing common core lesson plans, employing a subject matter coach, allocating more time for test preparation, enhancing the data tracking package, and/or adopting a common core teacher observation instrument.

As the school year progresses, various building and central office administrative staff will issue a progress report on the implementation of common core standards. Each report will reference some quantifiable component of the implementation process—number of workshops held, number of subjects adopting common core, number of consultants employed, scores on state tests. None of these reports will offer tangible evidence that students are making progress on the educational proficiencies listed in the common core standards:

- *Critical thinking*: the ability to analyze, evaluate, and problem-solve
- *Creative thinking*: the ability to generate, associate, and hypothesize
- *Complex thinking*: the ability to clarify, interpret, and determine
- *Comprehensive thinking*: the ability to understand, infer, and compare
- *Collaborative thinking*: the ability to explain, develop, and decide
- *Communicative thinking*: the ability to reason, connect, and represent

FOLLOWING THROUGH on Common Core

Educational mindsets begin the process of *following through* on common core with the assumption that this instructional initiative will transform how teachers think about and practice classroom teaching. When the goal shifts from implementation to transformation, administrators are drawn into a continuous learning process organized around three personal and administrative journeys (see figure 5.1).

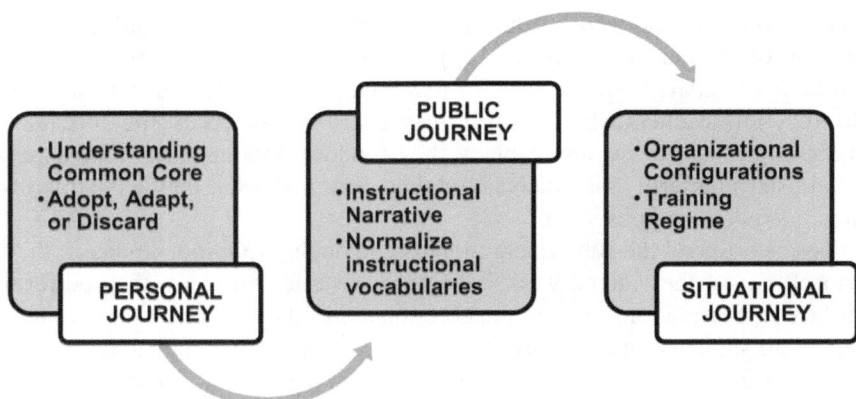

Figure 5.1 Following Through on Common Core.

The Personal Journey

The goal of this phase of following through is to develop a deep understanding of the context in which the common core would be implemented.

- Developing a personal understanding of the theories, concepts, and practices of common core.
- Based on that personal understanding, determining faculty readiness for successful implementation of common core (see Resource 2-8).
- Based on that personal understanding and the determination of faculty readiness, deciding whether to adopt all components of common core, adapt parts of common core, or put the implementation on hold until circumstances in the district or school bring common core into the zone of practicality.

The Public Journey

The goal of this phase of following through is to provide the school community with a rationale for adopting a new instructional initiative: WHAT is common core? WHY is common core important? HOW will we implement common core?

- Authoring an instructional narrative explaining the what, why, and how of common core (see Resource 5-1).
- Defining and employing the instructional vocabularies associated with common core (see Resource 5-2).

The Situational Journey

The goal of this phase of following through is to design organizational configurations that accommodate the activity structures of common core.

- Assembling organizational resources—time, space, materials, and expertise—to accommodate the activity structures of common core.
- Designing a training regime (see Resource 2-5) to help teachers apply the theories and practices of common core.

Once the school community agrees that common core is a good idea, school administrators must then create a learning environment where teachers are made to feel safe in a process that will take them beyond their instructional comfort zones (see figure 5.2).

Closing the gap between where teachers are coming from and where they need to be cannot be accomplished by sitting in main offices or by delegating the educational function to assistants. Living up to a school's mission statement is difficult because administrators must join with teachers to make collective sense out of theories and practices that will disrupt comfortable instructional routines.

There is inevitable stress and discord associated with adopting unfamiliar and untested instructional routines. A school administrator can only lessen this by occupying teacher workspaces and classrooms to identify and make the

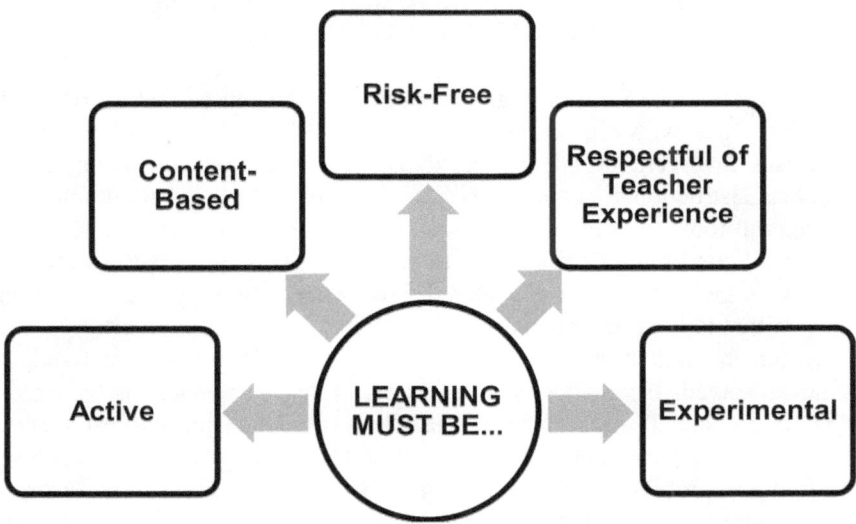

Figure 5.2 Principles of Adult Learning.

Table 5.3 Barriers to School Reform Initiatives

THE BARRIER	THE ADJUSTMENT
Resources	Time Materials Expertise
Organization	Schedules Space Instructional systems (employment, curriculum, teacher evaluation, assessment)
Understandings (Theories, Ideas, and Practices)	Adopt Adapt Discard
Accountability	Benchmarks Success criteria Timelines Evaluation instruments

necessary organizational and instruction adjustments (see table 5.3). In the case of common core, these adjustments might include employing another consultant, creating a new daily schedule, discarding selected standards, or authoring a new teacher evaluation instrument. Whatever frustrations inevitability arise within the final phase of *following through*, educational mindsets assume the responsibility for being present, being knowledgeable, and being decisive.

FOLLOWING THROUGH ON SCHOOL MISSION STATEMENTS

Within minutes of entering any main office, one senses that schools are very busy places. Main office calendars are filled with minute-by-minute responses to urgent problems caused by the malfunction of an organizational or instructional routine. School administrators employ the traditional managerial tools of adding a resource, writing a rule, employing additional personnel, purchasing a technology, or adjusting a system to fix the malfunction. An urgent problem is considered fixed when follow-up documentation is submitted to the proper department or agency.

Despite having documented that the urgent problem has been fixed, it is never solved. No matter what resources, rules, personnel, or technologies are employed, the problems of tardiness, absenteeism, low test scores, disobedience, fighting, class-cutting, and bullying always reappear. Each of these urgent problems are natural outgrowths of organizational and instructional regimes that prize institutional values over mission-driven values (see table 5.4).

Table 5.4 Institutional Values vs. Mission-driven Values

INSTITUTIONAL VALUES	MISSION-DRIVEN VALUES
Compliance	Agency
Standards	Interests
Rules	Relationships
Routines	Novelty
Conformity	Originality

Solving urgent schoolwide problems begins with the acknowledgment by administrators and teachers that the source of most urgent problems is the result of an unrealized mission-driven value. Fixing an urgent problem is not a matter of following up on implementation, but rather following through on the cultivation of mission-driven values.

RESOURCES

RESOURCE 5-1: Instructional Narrative for Adoption of Common Core Standards

Situation	This summer, all staff members received a packet of materials on the state mandate to adopt common core standards. Along with the state materials, I composed a one-page summary of our district's position on common core and how we would proceed to implement common core. After a summer of studying common core, speaking with university experts, and talking with many of you in the audience, I concluded that the adoption of common core would enhance the curriculum standards we are currently pursuing in the district. As you know, the district embarked on a five-year curriculum-writing project based on Deborah Meier's five habits of mind. We now have complete curriculum guides in three core subjects that contain objectives, activities, and assessments for each habit of mind. The goals and content of common core would align with what we have already written and would provide us with subject matter content and instructional strategies that would cultivate each habit of mind that we believe all students should possess when they graduate from our district.
Strategy	In my one-page summary, I listed the phases of implementation. I have sketched out tentative timelines for completing each phase of implementation. Phase I, which will be completed next year, is to complete the curriculum-writing process for all subjects. The final drafts will include areas where we believe we can integrate common core standards into the content and activity structures we have already established. Phase II of implementation will call upon our administrative team to redesign a number of organizational systems to accommodate the content demands and activity structures written into our curriculum guides. We may, for example, need to redesign our daily schedule to take into account activity structures that demand more class time, or we may have to relocate classrooms to accommodate team teaching formats. Phase III of implementation will involve all faculty in a training regime that will support teachers and administrators in a process to make collective sense out of the educational goals we established several years ago.
Capacity	As I stated two years ago, the educational goals our district decided to pursue were the right things to do for our students. At the same time, the goals we are pursuing present us with a very different teaching model than we have employed in this district. Understanding the theories behind this teaching model, and then practicing them in the classroom, will place all of us on a steep learning curve. I can assure you that our board is committed to these goals and will commit whatever resources we need to implement them. I am particularly pleased that last week, the board approved the contract for the services of Dr. Anna McCarthy. Anna will become our permanent instructional coach for the coming school year. I should add that the board also approved funding to pay teachers for participating in training and curriculum-writing projects. One final comment: the habits of mind curriculum and interdisciplinary programs are the number one priority of our board. They have instructed me not to permit any other mandates or initiatives to interfere with the educational goals they have written into our district strategic plan.

RESOURCE 5-2: The Vocabularies of Common Core

Grammar of Schooling	School Function	Common Core
Preparation for Occupational Role	*The goal is* . . .	Expansion of the intellect
Acquisition of Information	*Learning is* . . .	Construction of meaning
Delivering of Information	*Teaching is* . . .	Facilitation of understanding
The Technique of the Day	*Pedagogy is* . . .	Inquiry
State Standards	*Subject matter content is* . . .	Problems
Score on Standardized Test	*Performance is* . . .	Solutions to authentic problems

Chapter 6

The Crisis of the Day

> *Students need some tough love. We need to institute the three strikes (absent days) and you're out policy (dropped from class).*
>
> *(Teacher to Assistant Principal)*

Lou, attendance is awful this year. Each year attendance gets worse and worse. How do you expect us to raise test scores when our classrooms are half-empty each day? What happened to the recommendations of that attendance committee Dr. Smith formed last year? We need to stop making excuses for absenteeism. Students need some tough love. We need to institute the three strikes (absent days) and you're out policy (dropped from class).

FIXING PROBLEMS: THE BLAME GAME

School administrators begin every school year with well-rehearsed organizational and instructional routines designed to impose order on the behavior and education of large groups of children and adolescents. Within weeks of a new school year, however, a phone call from a parent, a memo from central office, a governmental mandate, a disciplinary infraction, or a number on a school report card will thrust main offices into situations that expose gaps between the educational ideals written into school mission statements and the practices of institutional schooling.

Most gaps between the *is* and *ought* of schooling are resolved with a managerial fix: add a resource, employ additional personnel, redesign a system, or write a new policy. There are disruptions that occur during a school year, however, that fail to respond to the application of routine managerial tools. When these failures surface, main offices are thrown into crisis mode.

Table 6.1 lists six typical examples of organizational and instructional disruptions that land in main office in-boxes each year. Each disruption is followed by an established managerial fix: add a resource (1, 3, and 4); redesign a system (2); adopt a program (5); or write a rule (6). With disruptions 1, 2, and 3, there is a high probability that managerial tools will fix the disruption. With disruptions 4, 5, and 6, there is a low probability that managerial tools will fix the disruption. In fact, in certain school situations, these managerial tools will worsen disruptions 4, 5, and 6.

When the undesirable disruptions of 4, 5, and 6 remain unresponsive to a managerial fix, managerial mindsets double down on institutional remedies—more resources, more rules, more personnel, or more technology. When doubling down fails to fix a schoolwide problem, managerial mindsets eventually blame one or more of the following individual or societal forces for failed institutional and instructional fixes:

It's the Student

Administrators and teachers collectively assume that a complex combination of inherited biological and cultural traits create dispositions, motivations, and behaviors that resist the rational policies, procedures, and practices of institutional schooling.

It's the Parent

Administrators and teachers collectively assume that a student's home life create dispositions, motivations, and behaviors that resist the rational policies, procedures, and practices of institutional schooling.

Table 6.1 Disruptions

DISRUPTION		MANAGERIAL FIX
1	Lack of textbooks	Order more textbooks
2	Overcrowded cafeteria	Balance student numbers
3	Large class sizes	Employ more teachers
4	High dropout rates for minority students	Employ a social worker
5	Low state testing math scores for minority students	Purchase a test preparation program
6	High truancy rates for minority students	Institute three strikes and you're out rule

It's the Organization

Administrators and teachers collectively assume that the resources provided by school organizations will never be adequate for overcoming student traits and home environments that resist the rational policies, procedures, and practices of institutional schooling.

It's Society

Administrators and teachers collectively assume that profound changes in the beliefs and values in society resist the rational policies, procedures, and practices of institutional schooling.

FIXING THE CRISIS OF THE DAY

Why do disruptions 4, 5, and 6 remain unresponsive to conventional managerial solutions? Disruptions 1, 2, and 3 all have clear objectives, clear cause-and-effect relationships, and clear outcomes. Each disruption involves an organizational category—materials, personnel, systems, or budget—that fits perfectly into managerial mindsets that are comfortable with telling, allocating, and inspecting. Disruptions 4, 5, and 6, however, involve a tangled web of social, cultural, and political variables that defy institutional efforts to identify, to describe, to categorize, and to regulate.

When these countless human, social, and cultural variables converge each day in hallways, they generate unpredictable and novel situations—the *crisis of the day*. Every institutional tool designed to impose order on these uncontrollable variables produces one or more of the following outcomes: the crisis of the day appears to be fixed; the crisis of the day becomes worse; or the crisis of the day reappears in a different form.

Each outcome is accompanied by a managerial explanation for successful or failed fixes to the crisis of the day. If a strategy appears to *fix the crisis* of the day, administrators point to a specific rule, procedure, system redesign, employment of personnel, or a technology as the remedy for the desired outcome. If the strategy fails *to fix* the crisis of the day, the blame game resumes. If the crisis of the day reappears in a different form, administrators declare the crisis as a new phenomenon requiring a different managerial strategy.

Performance in school administration is judged by how well the occupants of main offices fix the crisis of the day. The agenda of monthly board meetings is consumed with one administrator after another explaining one fix after another. While ticking off a list of managerial fixes, administrators are rarely asked why tardiness, absenteeism, bullying, drugs, and low test scores keep appearing on opening day agendas. The answer to that question entails a shift in thinking from a mindset intent on fixing the problems to a mindset intent on solving the problems.

> *"I know how to get these kids back to school, but you won't do it."*
> *(Truant Officer to Principal)*

"Sandy, are you aware of a group of freshman students who are not attending school on a regular basis?"

"Yes, I am."

"What are you doing about it?"

"I have followed the standard procedures of notifying and counseling truants."

"It appears from the reports on my desk that these standard procedures are not working."

"Dr. Jones, I can speak from experience that none of these measures will work."

"Well, Sandy, what works then?"

"Dr. Jones, I know how to get these students back to school, but you won't do it."

"What won't I do Sandy?"

"Dr. Jones, with all due respect, I know you care about these kids, but past administrators were unwilling to make the necessary changes to the school organization that would accommodate the needs of these students."

"Sandy, what changes to this school would bring these students back?"

"First, these students do not do mornings."

"Sandy, come on, what do you mean they don't do mornings?"

"They don't do mornings. Getting on a bus at 6:30 and sitting in a cafeteria until 8:00 just won't cut it with these students. They would be willing to come to school at 10:00, but not 8:00."

"What else?"

"They don't do gym."

"That's a state mandate."

"I told you that you wouldn't be able to accommodate these students."

"What else?"

"They want to study subjects they are interested in, not the required courses."

"Sandy, some of these required courses are state mandated. Go on."

"They do not navigate the seven-period school schedule very well. Ideally, they would be much more comfortable in some form of self-contained classroom with one or two teachers they get to know well."

"Anything else?"

"Dr. Jones, if you are really serious about this problem, I would be willing to come on board as a resource teacher for this program. Give me a classroom in the building annex. I will take responsibility for creating a curriculum and schedule that will accommodate the individual needs of these students."

"What about the gym and require courses mandate?"

"Dr. Jones, again with all due respect, that is your problem. I am just telling you what we need to do administratively and instructionally to bring these kids back to school."

SOLVING THE CRISIS OF THE DAY: FOOD FIGHTS IN THE CAFETERIA

Purchasing technologies, employing personnel, writing rules, and redesigning systems are managerial responses to simple organizational problems: a shortage of computers, a rise in class size, a need for regulation of cell phone use, or inaccurate grade reports. Each of these organizational problems has a clear cause-and-effect relationship and, for the most part, will be fixed with a managerial tool.

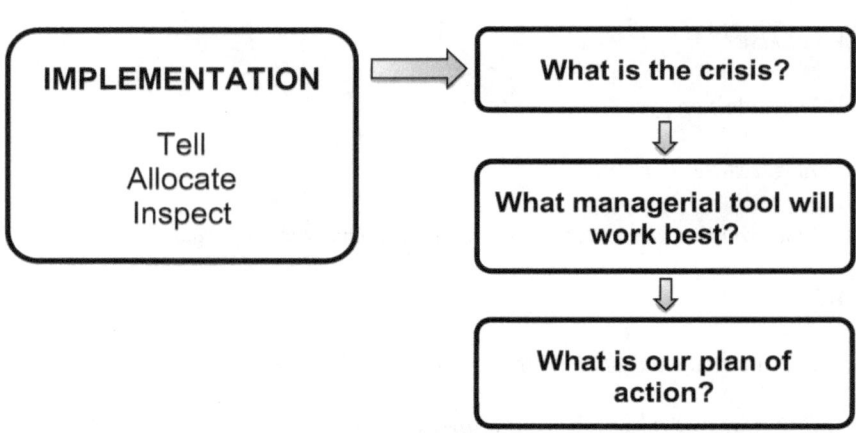

Figure 6.1 Fixing the Crisis of the Day.

These same managerial tools, however, are poorly suited for solving schoolwide learning and behavior problems. Installing additional computers will not raise student academic engagement. Employment of an additional dean will not increase student attendance. Purchasing a reading program will not increase student test scores. A managerial mindset focuses on the *what* and *how* of a problem and ignores the *why* of the problem, and as such, focuses on *implementation* (see figure 6.1).

Schools are complex organizations that defy the establishment of clear cause-and-effect relationships between school, society, the child, and the curriculum. Complex responses to schoolwide problems ask school administrators to orchestrate some form of an inquiry process beginning with asking the question: "Why does this schoolwide problem keep reappearing?" Asking the *why* question shifts attention from an implementation process to an inquiry/participation process: defining the problem→gathering and analyzing research on the problem→selecting an option to resolve the problem→developing a plan of action to implement the agreed-upon option→marshaling the appropriate resources to implement the option→and then adjusting agreed-upon strategies based on feedback from affected participants (see figure 6.2).

On the surface, recurring food fights in the cafeteria may appear to be a simple problem of catching the perpetuators and assigning a punishment. In certain school contexts, this managerial response might work. In other school contexts, the ignored variables present in the cafeteria will remain resistant to the simple response of catching and punishing. When catching and punishing fails to stop cafeteria disturbances, main offices are left with four administrative options:

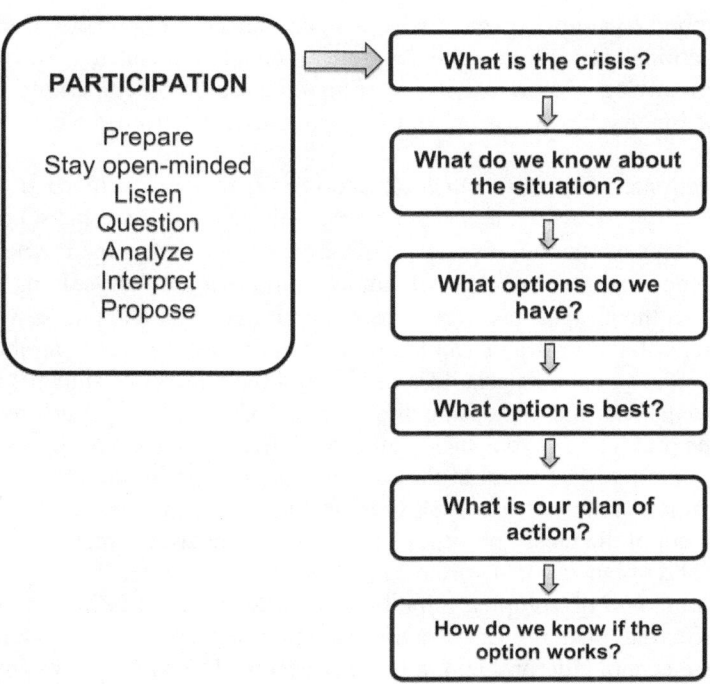

Figure 6.2 Solving the Crisis of the Day.

1. They can ignore the problem,
2. They can double down on a managerial fix,
3. They can launch the blame game, or,
4. They can treat the disturbance as a symptom of a far deeper problem in the design and implementation of established organizational routines.

Managerial mindsets are drawn to employing one or more of the managerial options 1, 2, and 3. Fixing the problem is reduced to the selection and implementation of a managerial tool. Educational mindsets, on the other hand, first determine if they are dealing with a simple or complex problem. Can the *why* of this problem—food fights in the cafeteria—be reduced to a clear relationship between cause and effect? If the disturbances are rare, the instigators are well known in the dean's office, and the outbreak occurs in the same period, then a managerial tool—catching and punishing—may fix the problem.

If, however, the outbreaks are a daily occurrence, involve large numbers of students, and show up in all of the lunch periods, the administrators may be dealing with a complex mix of cultural and organizational variables that will not respond to simple managerial fixes. The uncertainty, levels of training, organizational disruptions, and lengthy timelines associated with complex problem-solving discourage managerial mindsets from embarking on any form of inquiry beyond what tool they should select from their managerial toolbox.

Educational mindsets never look into their managerial toolbox or engage in an inquiry process without first understanding the nature of the schoolwide problem they are facing. If cafeteria disturbances are determined to be a complex phenomenon, an educational mindset initiates a problem-solving process that is part theory, part prediction, part experimentation, and part adjustment.

No school administrator can know for certain how selected variables will interact in a school cafeteria. Maybe limiting the number of students in each cafeteria period and increasing the number of supervisory personnel will solve the problem. Maybe placing an administrator in the cafeteria and reducing the number of minutes in the cafeteria period would solve the problem. The ultimate solution to complex organizational or instructional problems evolves out of the messy process of testing different arrangements of selected human and organizational variables (see Resource 6-1).

The outcome of complex thinking is a strategy representing an arrangement of variables that in a particular situation appears to work. Along with solving a schoolwide problem, a process designed to solve a complex problem will provide administrators and faculty with a tentative explanation of what caused the problem. After months of peaceful cafeteria periods, a school leader could return to his office knowing what particular instructional or organizational variables—increasing supervisory personnel or assigning an administrator to each cafeteria period—appear to have solved the problem. The only remaining unanswered question in the main office is whether the solution lived up to the educational goals and values written into the school's mission statement.

DOING THE RIGHT THING

The fundamental difference between fixing a problem and solving a problem is the same difference that exists between doing things right and doing the right thing. Organizations *do things right* when they implement well—they fix a problem. Organizations *do the right thing* when they add value to organization—they solve a problem. The distinction is an important one in organizations designed to achieve bureaucratic goals: speed, lack of ambiguity, continuity, uniformity, and discipline. Reducing the time students have for eating lunch or enforcing a silent lunch policy may restore order to the cafeteria. An institutional solution, however, may also reduce the quality of the lunchroom experience.

An educational mindset factors into their organizational and instructional strategies the answer to the valued-added question: "Are we doing the right thing?" (see Resource 6-2). In developing the right strategy for subduing cafeteria disturbances, administrators might include in their problem-solving conversations attention to what students valued most about cafeteria periods: the ability to talk freely, to move freely, and to eat freely.

Managerial fixes for a schoolwide problem ignore the value-added consideration: "How do children or adolescents feel about their lunchroom experience?" Managerial mindsets are motivated by achieving an institutional outcome—reducing lunchroom disturbances. Sitting quietly for an entire lunch period may be the price students must pay to achieve that institutional goal. While a managerial strategy may fix a schoolwide problem, organizational or instructional fixes that leave participants feeling helpless, angry, or confused serve as fertile ground for the reappearance of different strains of those same behaviors.

Educational mindsets ask value-added questions before they ask implementation questions. When the outcomes of a managerial strategy are found to degrade the quality of a school experience, educational administrators return to conference rooms and teacher workspaces to rethink the goals, methods, and outcomes of an agreed-upon solution to a schoolwide problem. At a minimum, the reexamination of an agreed-upon organizational or instructional strategy would include analyzing gaps between values listed in school mission statements and the outcomes of an agreed-upon strategy; reconsidering the theories, ideas, and practices formulating the strategy; redesigning the strategy to accommodate educational goals and values; and authoring new understandings of the what, why, and how of a redesigned strategy (see Resource 6-3).

THE ENTREPRENEUR

No matter how well-designed a strategy may be for solving messy classroom problems, the educational goals and values listed in school mission statements involve a complex web of political, cultural, social, and economic variables that established managerial tools are poorly designed to untangle.

While there is no fixed method of solving schoolwide organizational and instructional problems, dissecting the countless number of controllable and uncontrollable variables involved requires habits of thought and action described in this chapter. Even with habits of thought and action in place, the number and complexity of variables in play will produce a level of uncertainty that often constrains the kinds of necessary risk-taking involved in any solution to a complex schoolwide problem.

In the scenario that introduced this section, an administrator was offered a strategy for solving a worrisome truancy problem among a group of freshman students. The truancy officer presented the school administrator with a list of program specifications, that in her words, would bring these students back to school. Each specification, however, was either ignored or was in direct opposition to accepted organizational and instructional routines. In the words of the truant officer: "I know how to bring these kids back to school, but you won't do it."

What follows are the three scripts present in a main office wrestling with the complexities of bringing a group of truant students back to school.

Managerial Script

- *"I agree, I would like these students back in school."*
- *"I appreciate your passion."*
- *"You have some interesting ideas."*
- *"Unfortunately, in my position I have to pay attention to the rules and regulations."*
- *"We just don't have the resources you are asking for to address the problem."*
- *"I would ask that you follow the procedures we already have in place for truancy violations."*

Professional Script

- *"I knew he wouldn't do it."*
- *"Same old, same old—obey laws/no money."*
- *"Writing a letter to parents doesn't work."*
- *"Sending reports to the county doesn't work."*
- *"I know what works, but no one in any of these offices will do it."*

Entrepreneur's Script

- *"This is a bad situation—these kids need to be in school."*
- *"She is right, nothing we have done so far has worked."*
- *"She seems to know what she is talking about."*
- *"Not certain how I would handle some of the state mandates involved."*
- *"I have the room."*
- *"Money could be a problem . . . but these new truancy grants may cover it."*

The Crisis of the Day 105

- *"This won't work unless she is somehow in direct control of the program."*
- *"I'm calling the county. If I can get that grant money, this is doable."*

No mandate, rule, policy, procedure, program, technology, or specialist will solve the daily social, emotional, and intellectual struggles all young people experience in school. Nor will these things help a school live up to the abstract values, beliefs, and goals listed in school mission statements. Living up to the educational values and goals written into school mission statements will always call upon school administrators to step out of comfortable managerial roles and adopt the mindset of an *entrepreneur*.

What does the mindset of an entrepreneur look like? Resource 6-4 summarizes how managers, innovators, and entrepreneurs think about the daily problems and ideas that land in their main office in-boxes. The fundamental trait that sets entrepreneurs apart from managers and innovators is their ability to transform novel ideas into workable organizational routines. Managers are programmed to implement *what is*. Innovators are programmed to imagine *what could be*. Entrepreneurs are programmed to enact *what should be*.

Finding the right balance between accepted norms of institutional schooling and novel strategies for teaching and learning is what makes the entrepreneurial role so challenging. Entrepreneurial school administrators know that venturing too far outside of a school community's understandings of what institutional schooling should look like will doom any novel approach to teaching and learning. On the other hand, entrepreneurial school administrators also know that complex instructional and organizational problems in their schools will not be solved using traditional managerial and instructional scripts.

Daily school attendance, for example, is frequently cited in school mission statements as a valued educational goal. Returning to our truant freshman students, an entrepreneurial administrator would view this problem as a goal worth pursuing. From that commitment to a valued end of schooling, entrepreneurs assemble a strategy fashioned around the answer to the following realities of institutional schooling:

- *Does the proposed solution stem from sound theories and practices?*
- *Does the proposed solution fit well into the values, beliefs, and practices of the school community?*
- *Does the school organization possess the appropriate resources necessary to fully implement the proposed solution?*
- *Does the school organization possess the appropriate organizational structures to implement the proposed solution?*

No matter how intriguing a proposed solution may be, answering "no" to any one of these institutional realities would cause an entrepreneur to pause. A solution based on bad theory will fail to produce the promised outcomes. A solution that does not make sense to the school community will be resisted. A solution without proper resources will never realize the full potential of a theory or practice. A solution without a proper instructional and organizational infrastructure will not find pathways into classrooms and main offices.

Unless the entrepreneur in the main office is able to formulate a workaround for one or more of the realities of institutional schooling, the idea would be tabled. This does not mean the idea is dead. No good idea ever disappears in entrepreneurial main offices. They hang around in folders or on posted notes until the entrepreneur can confidently connect the implementation dots: right problem→right goals→right method→right people→right resources→right organizational structures. The essential trait of all entrepreneurial administrators is the continual search for configurations of schooling that open up possibilities for doing the right things.

The Crisis of the Day

RESOURCES

RESOURCE 6-1: Food Fights in the Cafeteria: Organizational and Cultural Variables

ORGANIZATIONAL VARIABLES		CULTURAL VARIABLES	
Design	Cafeteria layout creates blind spots	**Age**	Developmental level of students
Density	Population imbalances: some periods are overcrowded	**Ethnic Mix**	Cultural beliefs, values, habits of different ethnic groups in cafeteria
Supervision	Inadequate number and type of supervisory personnel	**Institutional**	What rules are valued and how are rules applied
Authority	No administrative personnel to hold supervisory personnel accountable	**Authority**	Age and ethnic response to authority
Time	Too much down time in period	**History**	Established patterns of acceptable and unacceptable behavior
Food	Cafeteria offerings are unappealing to children/adolescents	**Food**	Cafeteria offerings are unappealing to student populations being served

RESOURCE 6-2: Valued Ends of Schooling

THE VALUE	DEFINED	ORGANIZATIONAL RESPONSE
Intellectual (How do we examine life?)	True intelligence is not knowing all the answers, but knowing what questions to ask.	Teaching matters
Knowledgeable (How do we explain life?)	A professional knows the *what*, *why*, and *how* of what they are talking about.	Competence matters
Respectful (How do we treat each other?)	Children learn best in environments where diverse talent, abilities, and interests are known, respected, and nurtured.	Relationships matter
Skillful (How do we enact our values?)	Successful organizations do the small things well.	Execution matters
Thoughtful (How do we solve problems?)	Beliefs, judgments, and actions are supported by reasons and the evidence they provide.	Reasoning matters

RESOURCE 6-3: Adding Value to a School

STAGES	TASKS OF REDESIGNING
Reflecting	Are we meeting our criteria for successful performance? What gaps exist between criteria for successful performance and actual performance (valued-added cycle)? Why do these gaps exist? What is working? What is not working?
Reconnecting	What gaps exist between how we understood the problem and what we have learned about the problem? What theories, ideas, and practices should we reevaluate? What would the reinterpretation of our original theory-practice construct look like in our organization?
Rethinking	What changes to our building systems should we implement to address our new understandings of the instructional or organizational problem? What criteria for successful performance should we implement to evaluate our new understanding of the organizational or instructional problem? What tests/assessments will be employed to evaluate successful performance?
Reframing	What new vocabulary, concepts, and frameworks must we develop to describe and explain our new organizational/instructional strategy? What members of the school community should be informed of our new instructional/organizational strategy? What venues we will use to communicate our new instructional/organizational strategy?

RESOURCE 6-4: Managing, Innovating, Enacting

THE MANAGER Institutional Goals (Objectives + A Number)	THE ENTREPRENEUR Mission-Centered Goals (Vision + Desire + Objectives + A Number)	THE INNOVATOR Personalized Goals (Vision + Desire)
Outcomes	Criteria for Success	Processes
Hierarchies	Flat Structures	Networks
Best Practice	Best Model	Best Theory
Implement	Enact	Experiment
Risk-averse	Risk Management	Acceptable Risk
In Authority	Specialists	Is an Authority
Failure is Not an Option	Failure is Optimized	Failure is Expected
Solutions	Strategies	Questions
Strategies	Plans of Action	Hypotheses
Rule-bound	Breaks Rules	Author's New Rules

Chapter 7

Noticing

> *"Why are you standing outside of your classroom?"*
> *"I don't know. I might have been talking. He's always sending someone out of the room."*
>
> (Conversation between Principal and Student in Hallway)

THE NOISE AND THE SIGNS OF SCHOOLING

All organizations develop ways of arranging work that align with the goals and functions they perform. Schools are organizations designed to house, move, and document the educational progress of large groups of students. This "institutional schooling" prioritizes smooth operations above all else. Self-contained classrooms, bell schedules, subjects, departments, specialists, report cards, and main offices are all components of an organization designed to impose certainty on inherently uncertain populations and uncertain processes. A late bus, a bell that does not ring, grades not handed in, groups of students congregating in a hallway, graffiti in a washroom, or a classroom without a teacher, are all disruptions to organizational and instructional routines that draw the *notice* of managerial mindsets.

Each of these disruptions to the norms of institutional schooling represent the noise of schooling. School administrators are largely judged by how adept they are at silencing that noise. However, in silencing the noise of schooling, administrators do not notice the signs that the school is not living up to the educational values listed in school mission statements. Is a student standing outside of a classroom during a period the noise of adolescent misbehavior or a sign that learners are not being engaged in meaningful learning experiences? Is graffiti in the washroom the noise of juvenile vandalism or a sign of a gang presence? Is an accident report the noise of adolescent carelessness or the sign of an unsafe school environment? Is a parent complaint the noise of special interest or the sign of indifference to the unique social, emotional, and intellectual needs of students?

If signs pose the real threats to the goals and values listed in a school's mission statement, why do these signs go unnoticed in main offices? What follows are five fundamental managerial beliefs housed in main offices that act as powerful firewalls against noticing the signs of schooling.

Certainty

Managerial mindsets are most comfortable with supervising the certain routines of allocating, assigning, scheduling, staffing, planning, and organizing. This same mindset is uncomfortable when asked to make decisions in a situation where the goals are unclear, the causes are unclear, and knowledge is incomplete. Administrators who notice signs are drawn into ambiguous situations that do not respond to managerial fixes such as adding a resource, writing a rule, or redesigning a system.

Truth

Managerial mindsets are most comfortable with supervising the certain truths of policies, procedures, rules, and routines. This same mindset is uncomfortable when asked to choose between competing theories, competing sources of information, and competing strategies. Administrators who notice signs are drawn into deciding upon what truth is hiding behind the noise of institutional schooling.

Values

Managerial mindsets are most comfortable with supervising the institutional values of efficiency, competence, and responsiveness. This same mindset is uncomfortable in situations where they are asked to determine what valued ends of schooling to pursue. Administrators who notice signs are drawn into articulating and promoting the educational beliefs and values written into district and school mission statements.

Time

Managerial mindsets are most comfortable with checking off tasks listed on their daily "to do" lists. Each task on the list prescribes specific timelines that align with one or more managerial functions—telling, allocating, or inspecting. This same mindset is uncomfortable in situations where processes involve educational functions—educating, facilitating, and coaching. Administrators who notice signs are drawn into developing an educational process where each educational function resists the establishment of firm timelines.

Disruption

Managerial mindsets are most comfortable with regulating established organizational and instructional routines—"if it is not broken, don't fix it." Disruptions to these organizational and instructional routines are fixed with minor managerial adjustments to a budget, a schedule, a technology, a human resource, or a system. This same mindset is uncomfortable in situations asking them to disrupt established beliefs, values, and practices. Administrators who notice signs are drawn into a complex process of designing an instructional or organizational regime that would transform the noise of institutional norms into a sign of living up to a school's mission statement.

> *"Jeff, please come by after school today. I would like to talk to you about a conversation I had with a student outside of your room."*
>
> *(Principal to Teacher)*

NOTICING VALUES

What transforms a noisy institutional process into an educational sign is noticing the link between a schoolwide problem and an educational value listed in a school mission statement. Noticing a schoolwide disruption as a *sign* of an endangered educational value is necessary but not sufficient for living up to a school's mission statement. The leadership and managerial actions that an administrator initiates after noticing a schoolwide disruption for what it is—a sign—determine whether an educational value will be achieved or will merely remain an abstraction written into a school's publicity pamphlet.

Table 7.1 lists common events in school that draw the notice of school administrators. Embedded in each event are educational and organizational values listed in school mission statements. A school administrator could treat each event as merely the noise of schooling. Traditional managerial tools—adding a resource, writing a rule, or adopting a program—will appear to address the situation. While a managerial tool may reduce the noise of the situation, the opportunity to enact a valued end of schooling will be lost.

School administrators who choose to *notice* a missing educational value in a situation will be drawn into a messy problem-solving and implementation process described in chapter 6. The length of time involved in these processes,

Table 7.1 Noticing Values

WHAT GETS NOTICED	VALUE	RESPONSE TO NOISE	RESPONSE TO THE SIGN
Perfunctory monthly faculty meetings	**Collaboration**	Reduce number of faculty meetings	Foster learning communities
Rise in Absenteeism	**Caring Environment**	Increase penalty for nonattendance	Develop student advisory period
Parent concern over amount and mindlessness of homework	**Meaningful Learning Experiences**	Purchase new computers	Develop interdisciplinary periods
Yearly career day	**Lifelong Learning**	Sponsor career day	Develop problem-based learning units
Rise in Hispanic Dropouts	**Diversity**	Sponsor multicultural day	Develop bilingual program
National survey on student civic knowledge	**Responsible Citizenship**	Invite local elected officials to speak to classes	Develop "Legislative Assembly" simulation

along with the very real possibility of unclear outcomes, often deters main offices from seeing signs in the noise of schooling. Connecting values with administrative practices, however, is the very definition of leadership: every sign offers an opportunity to reinforce the values of what an educational organization stands for—living up to a school's mission statement.

Chapter 8

Tools in the Toolbox

> *"You didn't miss anything at the summer workshop. Two full days of a consultant telling us how to teach the district's new mathematics program. How my third graders are going to understand what she called 'conceptual mathematics' is beyond me."*
>
> *(Teacher Conversation on Opening Day)*

"You didn't miss anything at the summer workshop. Two full days of a consultant telling us how to teach the district's new mathematics program. How my third graders are going to understand what she called 'conceptual mathematics' is beyond me. I barely understood where she was going half the time."

"Sounds, awful. Last night, I did take a look at the curriculum binder for the program. My minor was mathematics, but I agree with you: this kind of math is well beyond the grade level I teach."

"At the end of the workshop, Dr. James kept referring to a pacing chart we need to hand in each week and the observation protocols that principals will use in classroom observations."

"After lunch, would it be alright if I came over to your room and went over the chart and protocols?

"No problem. In fact, our entire grade level team is getting together to discuss the chart and protocols."

Chapter 8

THE CYCLE OF REFORM FAILURE

Every school year begins with administrators on stages announcing a new initiative to achieve one or more of the educational goals listed in school mission statements. By November, the resources announced to help administrators and teachers develop a deep understanding of a new teaching model have been diverted to achieve the managerial goals of complying, standardizing, and documenting. Without the materials, space, time, or expertise to fully develop an understanding of the theories, concepts, and practices of a new teaching model, administrators and teachers reduce the substance of the new instructional initiative to procedural representations that are easily observed and documented. The reform cycle ends at the end of the school year with the submission of the appropriate forms verifying compliance with the procedural representations of the reform initiative. During the summer months, the reform cycle starts up again, with administrators gathering in conference rooms to consider, and then adopt, a new program, a new mandate, a new policy, a new rule, a new test, a new teaching model, or a new technology.

The comings and goings of programs and mandates reflect a school organization with no educational identity. Managerial mindsets see nothing wrong with supervising yearly initiatives that are disjointed and value-free. Implementing the particulars of a mandate, a policy, or a program (announcing, distributing, and documenting) is what matters most in managerial main offices. In meetings devoted to budgets, timelines, schedules, workshops, and documentation, no one voices concerns about whether the particulars of a new initiative make collective sense to staff or agree with the educational goals written into school mission statements. The organizational tools employed by managerial mindsets reflect valuing the goal of implementation over the goal of collective sensemaking (see Resource 8-1).

Educational mindsets view the authoring of a distinct educational identity as the essential vehicle to break the cycle of reform failure. Without a coherent and continuous commitment to an instructional worldview—how children learn—the development of the deep understandings necessary to practice new theories and strategies is lost within a maze of confused and often opposing programs and techniques of the day. Developing and enacting an agreed-upon instructional worldview draws school administrators into meetings devoted to theory and practice talk. The organizational tools employed by educational mindsets reflect valuing the goal of collective sensemaking over implementation (see Resource 8-2).

The cycle of reform failure is triggered by the competing goals and practices of these two administrative mindsets: managerial mindsets desire to preserve familiar organizational tools and educational mindsets desire to force administrators and teachers to adopt unfamiliar educational tools. School

Table 8.1 Doing the Right Things Well

"DOING THINGS RIGHT" (Managing) The WHO and HOW of Schooling	"DOING THE RIGHT THINGS" (Purposing) The WHY and WHAT of Schooling
Emphasizes PARTICIPATION	Emphasizes PERFORMANCE
Handles SITUATIONS	Provides SYMBOLS and enhances MEANING
Emphasizes PLANNING	Emphasizes PURPOSING
Gives DIRECTIONS	Builds CAPACITY
Builds MONITORING systems	Builds ACCOUNTABILITY systems
EXTRINSIC MOTIVATION (Carrots and Sticks)	INTRINSIC MOTIVATION (Meaning, Trust, Commitment, Identity, Efficacy)
CONGENIALITY	COLLEGIALITY
Creates LOGICAL PATTERNS	Creates COGNITIVE DISSONANCE

reform is not an either/or proposition; it is a both/and undertaking. Without the organizational tools—telling, allocating, and inspecting—administrators lack the processes and capacity to incorporate new theories and practices into established institutional structures; without the educational tools—educating, facilitating, and coaching—administrators and teachers lack the processes to make collective sense out of new theories and practices.

Table 8.1 summarizes the relationship between the managerial function of school policy manuals and the purposing function of school mission statements. Incorporated in each educational function is a managerial function: gathering the right materials and personnel (building capacity) will include some degree of ordering (giving direction); creating a compelling instructional narrative (purposing) will include some degree of planning; designing success criteria (building accountability systems) will include some degree of monitoring.

> *"How was the workshop this summer?" "All I can say is the district is serious about the new math program they adopted last year. The Superintendent laid out her vision and rationale for moving from plug and chug math to concept-based mathematics."*
>
> *(Teacher Conversation on Opening Day)*

"How was the workshop this summer?"

> *"All I can say is the district is serious about the new math program they adopted last year. The Superintendent laid out her vision and rationale for moving from plug and chug math to concept-based mathematics. Dr. James then spent considerable time reviewing the details of this year's staff development program."*

"What does that look like?"

"Our team meetings have been lengthened. Each grade level has been assigned a math coach. Each week we will have a half-day workshop to assist us with any difficulties we are having with the math content. The coaches and consultants will participate in joint planning sessions."

"How will we be evaluated?"

"Principals are not observing math sessions. Our math classes will be observed two or three times a week by our math coaches. These observations will be the focus of our team meetings."

PUTTING THE TOOLS TOGETHER

Managerial mindsets devote all of the institutional tools at their disposal—budgets, personnel, time, materials, space, and systems—to the tasks of telling, allocating, and inspecting. School administrators living up to their school's mission statement devote these same institutional tools to the tasks of educating, facilitating, and coaching. Each of these learning functions fits into a pattern of managerial and instructional moves that generate a continuous process of collective sensemaking.

The continual movement of the knowledge cycle is entirely dependent on the ability of school administrators to connect the educational tools of collective sensemaking to the organizational tools of implementation. Table 8-2 summarizes the managerial and educational tools a school administrator orchestrates to connect the educational mission of schooling to the organizational realities of institutional schooling.

While each of these organizational and educational tools are necessary, they are not sufficient for organizing instructional theories and practices designed to live up to a school's mission statement. The knowledge cycle is fashioned around a school administrator's adeptness at joining theoretical abstractions to classroom realities (see Resource 8-3). All vocabularies and behaviors of mission-driven administrators continually model and articulate the connection between the what and why of schooling—vision→worldview→knowledge—to the how and who of schooling—context→capacity→narrative. When done well, living up to a school's mission statement is a purposeful process of creating a meaningful association between a school's educational identity and a school's organizational reality.

Table 8.2 Connecting the What, Why, and How

Tools for EDUCATING	Tools for MANAGING	Tools for ENACTING
Instructional worldview	Goals/objectives	Personnel assignments
Curriculum development	Policies, procedures, schedules, flowcharts, job descriptions	Workflow patterns
Professional development	Budgets	Communication flow networks
Teacher evaluation	Assessment indicators	Resource assignments
Employment protocols	Patterns of authority and responsibility	Measurements
Mentoring	Materials	Data analysis
Habits of thought	Revisions of theories, goals, and processes based on gaps between success indicators and actual performance	Systems adjustments based on measurements and data
Vocabularies		Assessment of newly developed policies, procedures, and flowcharts

RESOURCES

RESOURCE 8-1: Tasks of Implementation

ACTS OF PLANNING	ORGANIZATIONAL CONFIGURATIONS
Develop goals and objectives	Distribute mandate, policy, or directive
Develop budget, managerial tasks, and establish timelines	Schedule meeting to develop a plan of action and assign administrative responsibilities and tasks
Develop written policies, procedures, schedules, flowcharts, and job descriptions	Schedule meeting to review policies, procedures, schedules, flowcharts, and job descriptions
Assign and schedule materials and personnel	Monitor the distribution of resources and timelines for completion of managerial tasks
Conduct measurement of assessment indicators	Review established data points for project completion
Adjust goals and plans of action	Schedule meetings to review performance data

RESOURCE 8-2: Tasks of Collective Sensemaking

ACTS OF INTERPRETATION	ORGANIZATIONAL TOOLS
Disrupt normative understandings of an instructional problem	Provide time, expertise, and materials to experiment, interpret, and practice a new pedagogy
Introduce new vocabularies, theories, and practices governing an instructional problem	Provide safe spaces for teachers to fail with a new pedagogy
Explain and model new vocabularies, theories, and practices in teacher workspaces	Provide venues where teachers clarify and challenge habits of teaching
Become a participant in instructional conversations around problems evolving out of the implementation of a new pedagogy	Provide technical and logistical support for teachers struggling with a new pedagogy

Reprinted by permission of the Publisher. From Alan C. Jones, *Becoming a Strong Instructional Leader: Saying No to Business as Usual,* New York: Teachers College Press. Copyright © 2012 by Teachers College, Columbia University. All rights reserved.

RESOURCE 8-3: The Cycle of Knowledge

	Vision	A well-articulated response to the question: Why are we here?
	Instructional Worldview	A coherent pedagogical framework best suited to achieve a schoolwide vision
	Knowledge	A thorough understanding and application of the theories and practices composing a school's instructional worldview
	Context	A thorough grasp of the cultural, political, and economic realities of a school community
	Capacity	A realistic assessment of the available organizational tools—personnel, materials, systems, and time—to implement a schoolwide vision
	Narrative	A well-crafted instructional narrative describing the what, why, and how of a schoolwide vision

Chapter 9

Getting to YES

> "Ms. James, as you know, all the schools in the district have experienced budget cuts. We just do not have the funds to support a half-time university consultant. The district is reassigning some central office personnel that may be able to fill that role."
>
> (Principal to Teacher)

INSTITUTIONAL NOS

Members of the school community continually ask administrators for decisions on the interpretation and implementation of *organizational* and *instructional* policies, procedures, and practices. These requests fall into three categories: rules, procedures, or materials. Administrators are asked: to interpret the goals and meaning of laws, policies, mandates, directives, or programs *(rules);* to change a protocol, schedule, system, or routine *(procedures);* or to add additional personnel, space, time, or materials *(materials)*.

Managerial mindsets respond to these requests with three institutional responses:

- We must comply . . .
- We cannot change . . .
- We do not have . . .

Rarely do teachers become upset with these institutional responses. They have come to expect that asking administrators to redesign organizational routines to accommodate new approaches to teaching and learning will be

Table 9.1 Institutional Nos

THE ISSUE	THE CONTENT	THE INSTITUTIONAL NO
Rules	• Law • Policy • Mandate • Directive • Program	Dr. Smith, the scope and sequence chart for the new math program is leaving out several topics which fourth graders will need next year. Ms. James, the content of the new math program is aligned with the state testing program. As you know, a board goal this year is to raise our scores in reading and mathematics. Our consultants recommend that this program aligns best to state standards.
Procedures	• Protocol • Schedule • System • Routine	Dr. Smith, we need common meeting times to coordinate the activities in the new math program. Ms. James, we added another period of reading, which limits our ability to free up time in the schedule for common meeting times.
Materials	• Personnel • Space • Time • Materials	Dr. Smith, would it be possible to bring back that university consultant we had during the summer math workshops? Her ability to model the concepts in the program was very helpful. Ms. James, as you know, all the schools in the district have experienced budget cuts. We just do not have the funds to support a half-time university consultant. The district is reassigning some central office personnel that may be able to fill that role.

met with an institutional NO. Table 9.1 illustrates the thinking and narrative behind each institutional NO.

The same cannot be said about *institutional* requests. Any rule, procedure, or resource that touches on an institutional goal or practice will receive the necessary latitude in meaning, procedures, and resources to implement the prescribed goal or practice. Figure 9.1 shows institutional adoptions that touch upon educational goals and values. Each adoption will be translated into managerial means and ends by managerial mindsets.

Each of the requests above was reduced to the implementation of a managerial tool: extended time, purchase of materials, employment of personnel, or installation of a technology. Each managerial response provided administrators with tangible actions and outcomes that demonstrated the implementation of a mandate, a program, or rule. None of these tangible managerial actions—employing, purchasing, or installing—describe how these managerial tools will be applied to achieve an educational goal or value written into a school mission statement. When teachers question the *how* of implementation—more time, more assistance, or more training—the response is an *institutional no*.

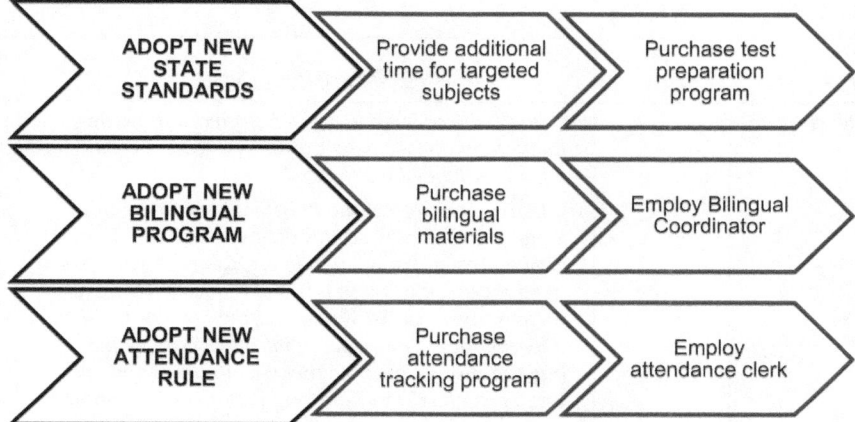

Figure 9.1 Managerial Means and Ends.

GETTING TO YES

> *Ms. James, I agree we need professional help with the new math program. We are strapped for funding, but I am working out an agreement with Dr. Marshall to work with our staff on the math program in exchange for a possible research paper on the project.*
>
> (Principal to Teacher)

Administrators living up to their school mission statements find ways of getting around institutional no responses—*getting to yes*. Table 9.2 illustrates how school administrators are able to transform an institutional constraint—time, money, or schedules—into an educational opportunity. In each of the cases below, school administrators authored strategies to find space within the institutional no for an educational yes. No matter what the social context of the school may be, there always exist sources of funding, access to expertise, flexibility in scheduling, availability of space, and gradations of compliance that can be creativity employed to help realize educational goals and values.

Admittedly, getting to yes will push administrators out of their managerial comfort zone. It is more comfortable to tell, to comply, and to deny than to listen, to reinterpret, and to invent. Administrators deciding to get to an educational yes will have to reacquire the managerial skills summarized below that often atrophy in main offices guided by institutional goals and values.

Table 9.2 Getting to Yes

THE ISSUE	THE CONTENT	GETTING TO YES
Rules	Law Policy Mandate Directive Program	Dr. Smith, the scope and sequence chart for the new math program is leaving out several topics which fourth graders will need next year. Ms. James, you are not the only teacher to raise this issue. I have expressed this concern with the District Office. As you know, in the past, Central Office has not been receptive to these types of requests. However, I made some calls last week, and the head of the math department at Governors State is willing to come out and discuss possible revisions to the scope and sequence chart. I will use some left-over funds from our school improvement grant to fund these after-school sessions.
Procedures	Protocol Schedule System Routine	Dr. Smith, we need common meeting times to coordinate the activities in the new math program. Ms. James, I agree that this math program is far more complex than I anticipated. Please be patient. All this week, I am meeting with the team leaders from each subject to see where we can get time for common planning periods. I've invited Jim from data processing to sit in on the meetings. He knows the master schedule in and out. If anyone can figure out a way to get common meeting times in our schedule, it is Jim.
Materials	Personnel Space Time Materials	Dr. Smith, would it be possible to bring back that university consultant we had during the summer math workshops? Her ability to model the concepts in the program was very helpful. Ms. James, I agree we need professional help with new math program. We are strapped for funding, but I am working out an agreement with Dr. Marshall to work with our staff on the math program in exchange for a possible research paper on the project.

Listening

There is a wide gap in thinking and practices between classrooms designed to educate and main offices designed to institutionalize. Classrooms make every effort to individualize, to interest, and to grow. Main offices make every effort to standardize, to comply, and to certify. The incompatibility of these goals is resolved with a silent agreement between teachers and administrators that "if you don't bother me, I won't bother you." What this agreement looks like in practice is the simple understanding that teachers will comply with all managerial procedures and accountability outcomes in exchange for administrators staying away from the inner workings of classrooms. A provision in this truce is the willingness of teachers to accept, without question, an institutional no.

Administrators will be unable to get to yes unless they completely understand the obstacles teachers experience in attempting to live up to educational goals and values written into school mission statements. For administrators, that means breaking the truce, entering teacher workspaces, and listening to what teachers say about their classrooms' experiences. Every school has different obstacles to living up to its mission statement. Maybe the obstacle is insufficient time, maybe it is insufficient training, maybe it is too many students, or maybe there is a lack of technology. Each *maybe* must be taken seriously, must be prioritized, and must be addressed in some managerial form. Teachers will be willing to commit to understanding and practicing new instructional models only if they feel that someone in the main office is listening. Getting to yes means getting out of your office, getting into classrooms, and listening to teachers.

Learning

All new organizational or instructional initiatives involve theories, ideas, and practices that will be foreign to staff and faculty. For the staff and faculty to become comfortable with foreign theories, ideas, and practices, administrators must possess the knowledge and skills to help the school community make collective sense of the substance of the new instructional model. At a minimum, making collective sense out of foreign theories, ideas, and practices will involve an instructional narrative outlining the what, why, and how of implementation; an interpretation of the meaning and application of theories, ideas, and concepts; a training regime designed to align with the substance and level of complexity of new instructional initiative; and a plan for restructuring the school organization to accommodate the implementation of a new instructional model.

These prerequisites for making collective sense out of foreign theories, ideas, and practices require a deep understanding of the substance of the new instructional initiative. Getting to yes means getting knowledgeable.

Testing

All new instructional models will generate countless known and unknown social, political, economic, and intellectual variables. Some of these variables are controllable; others are not. Some of the variables will interact in predictable ways; others will not. No matter how much thought goes into the implementation of a new instructional initiative, the number of uncontrollable variables involved will always produce unanticipated outcomes. Managerial mindsets sidestep the uncertainties of implementing new instructional models by focusing attention on variables that can be known, labeled, scheduled, and documented. Educational mindsets confront the uncertainties of implementing new instructional models head on by participating in a continuous process of planning, doing, checking, and acting. Getting to yes means getting comfortable with trial and error.

Guarding

The educational worth of a new mandate or program becomes diluted in main offices when it fails to align with an agreed-upon model of teaching and fails to align with the goals, theories, and practices of reform initiatives that have previously been implemented. Developing a robust understanding of new pedagogical theories, concepts, and practices is a cumulative process. Teachers are immersed in a years-long staff develop a program designed to develop a collective understanding of the what, why, and how of a new pedagogical model. Mandates, programs, policies, and procedures that disrupt

Table 9.3 How Administrators Stay the Course

They Comply	All new mandates, programs, policies, and procedures include a variety of accountability tools to document the implementation of a new initiative.
	Administrators living up to their schools' mission statements prevent diversion from the substance of a new reform initiative by making certain the school is in full compliance with the procedural requirements of the mandate, program, policy, or procedure.
They Interpret	The substance of a new school reform initiative will contain theories, concepts, practices, and vocabularies that are open to interpretation.
	Administrators living up to their schools' mission statements author an interpretation of the mandate, program, policy, or procedure that aligns with the school's instructional worldview and applies the theories, concepts, and practices of an adopted pedagogical model.
They Ignore	School offices are busy places. Along with the accountability and operational wants of governmental agencies, there is a long list of operational needs that must be addressed each year.
	Administrators living up to their schools' mission statements pay close attention to the yearly priorities established by outside agencies and central offices. A new mandate, program, policy, or procedure that disappears from meeting agendas, governmental directives, or central office memoranda can be safely ignored.
They Disobey	There are mandates, programs, policies, or procedures that will do great harm to the emotional, social, and intellectual development of young people.
	Administrators living up to their schools' mission statements develop a rationale for rejecting a mandate, program, policy, or procedure that jeopardizes one or more goals or values written into school mission statements.

the process of continuous improvement create a hesitancy among teachers to experiment with new pedagogical theories, concepts, and practices. School administrators choosing to live up to the goals and values in their school mission statements employ the managerial strategies in table 9.3 to safeguard the continuity and coherence of a professional learning process. Getting to yes means staying the course.

CREATING VALUE IN YOUR SCHOOL ORGANIZATION

Each day in main offices, school administrators have the choice to give the institutional no or to get to yes. Managerial mindsets favor the instrumental certainty of saying no. Educational mindsets favor the expressive uncertainties of saying yes. In the end, choosing whether to live up to the educational mission of schooling or to satisfy the managerial realities of institutional schooling becomes a question of values: What goals and practices add value to your organization? What goals and practices subtract value from your school organization?

The managerial tools employed to implement institutional goals and practices—rules, procedures, systems, job descriptions, certification, schedules, credits, courses, and standardized testing—are specifically designed to limit the movement, thinking, methodologies, monies, and performances of teachers and students. These tools subtract educational value from the school organization.

The educational tools employed to live up to the educational goals and values written into school mission statements—staff development, curriculum development, mentoring, learning communities, interdisciplinary course offering, interactive technologies, authentic assessments, and problem-based learning—are specifically designed to expand the movement, thinking, methodologies, monies, and performances of teachers and students. These tools create educational value in the school organization.

No mandate, program, policy, procedure, or rule is a neutral order. All organizational and governmental orders can be interpreted and applied in ways that either subtract or add educational value. The decision to give the institutional no maximizes the efficiencies of servicing large groups of students. The decision to get to yes maximizes the capacities to properly service the individualities of student bodies. The decision to subtract or create value in a school organization will reflect how faithful a school community will be to the educational goals and values written into a school's mission statement.

Chapter 10

Restoring the Why to Schooling

> *"I have a growing conviction that what's needed is not just more programs, but a larger purpose, a larger sense of mission . . ."*
> (Ernest L. Boyer, 1996)

At some point early on in the school year, all teachers will be asked by a student—usually seated in the back of the classroom—the fundamental question of schooling: "Why are we studying this subject?" Variations on this question are

"This subject is so boring!"

"Is this movie day?"

"Is this a required subject?"

"Can I have a pass to the bathroom?"

Most teachers provide institutional responses to these why questions:

"You need this subject to get into college."

"This subject is a prerequisite course for..."

"You need this course to get a good job."

At some point early on in the school year, all administrators will be asked by a teacher—usually seated in the back of darken auditorium: "Why are we starting a new program?" Variations on this question are:

"Didn't we do this program three years ago?"

"What about the program we started last year?"

"Are we going to get release time for training?"

"Do we have to complete all of those forms at the end of the year?"

Most administrators provide institutional answers to these why questions:

"Yes, we have a lot on our plate, but this program is state-mandated."

"We will use our scheduled four half-day institute days for training."

"Our new data management system will reduce the amount of paperwork involved."

At some point early on in the school year, all Superintendents will be asked by a principal, usually seated at the end of a conference table: "Why do we keep adopting a new program every year?" Variations on this question are:

"Do we have the resources to implement this program?"

"What about the program we adopted last year?"

"Will our current schedule accommodate the recommended minutes for this program?"

Most Superintendents provide institutional answers for these why questions:

"If our school improvement grant is approved, we should have adequate funding for the program."

"We are in compliance with last year's state mandate."

"Data processing has informed me that our schedule is now locked in. We are looking at making up the minutes in our advisory periods."

At no point in these *why* conversations does someone reference the *why* document published by all school districts: the schools' mission statements. The annual administrative ritual of distributing mission statements to teaching staff is followed up by the annual teacher ritual of laying to rest the why of schooling at the bottom of file cabinets, desk draws, or the recycle bins outside of auditorium doors.

THE DILEMMA OF INSTITUTIONAL SCHOOLING

In schools where managerial mindsets control main offices, priority is given to the efficient implementation of institutional functions: credentialing, accreditation, standardization, regulation, and accounting. While these institutional functions effectively control student behavior and some student outcomes, they are poorly suited for developing the diverse talents, abilities, and interests of students. The principal difference between each set of goals is how managers and educators answer the question: *Why are we here?*

Managerial responses to the question of the *why* of schooling are populated with vocabularies that emphasize organizational structures. Educational responses to the question of the *why* of schooling are populated with vocabularies that emphasize human agency. Each orientation represents a bundle of ideas, beliefs, and practices: a mindset that is either managerial or educational. Table 10.1 presents a summary of the clash between school structures designed to ensure uniformity, predictability, and obedience and mission statements that promote freedom, creativity, and autonomy.

Organizational structures and instructional regimes that are fundamentally opposed to the educational goals and values written into school mission statements create a dilemma for administrators wanting to live up to those mission statements. Faced each day with the dilemma of institutional schooling, school administrators have three choices: retreat to main offices to carry out managerial functions; carry out surface representations of educational goals and values; or shape and implement a vision of schooling that lives up the educational goals and values written into school mission statements.

Each chapter in this book describes the thinking and practices of school administrators who are working to restore the *why* to classroom instruction. The *how* of these strategies is driven by school administrators who practice the art of *Eclectic Leadership*.

Table 10.1 The Dilemma of Institutional Schooling

ELEMENT OF SCHOOLING	INSTITUTION-DRIVEN	MISSION-DRIVEN
Goals	Accountability	Responsibility
Human Experience	Standardized	Novel
Human Judgment	Rational/Logical Thinking	Practical Wisdom
Learning	Preparation	Meaningfulness
Teaching	Science	Art
Achievement	Performance	Mastery
Authority	Positional	Relational
Excellence	Maximize Talent	Optimize Talent
Outcomes	Quantifiable	Qualifiable
School Improvement	Prescriptive	Reflective
Curriculum Development	Alignment	Understanding
Instructional Leadership	Implementation	Collective Sensemaking

Chapter 10
ECLECTIC LEADERS

School reform advocates all agree upon the vital role school leadership plays in the successful implementation of school reform agendas. Although there are varying profiles of what this leadership should look like in schools, there is common agreement over the emphasis and conduct of school administrators: occupants of main offices should be filling their calendars with activities directly related to the enactment of the educational goals and values listed in school mission statements. These same profiles are clear about what school administrators should *not* be spending most of their office time on: managerial functions associated with operating a school organization.

When surveyed, school administrators overwhelmingly agree with school reformers on the importance and functions of instructional leadership. After completing the surveys, however, most school administrators return to daily calendars packed with managerial functions. Powerful social, political, and organizational forces pull school administrators away from the educational functions of instructional leadership. If presented with the reform option of pursuing managerial or educative goals, school administrators will choose the certainties of implementing managerial functions and overlook the uncertainties of enacting abstract educational concepts.

School administrators do not have to choose between managerial means or educational ends. Eclectic leaders enter main offices with the understanding that institutional schooling is here to stay—school communities expect their schools to be safe, to follow expected organizational and instructional routines, and to properly document the academic progress of their sons or daughters. At the same time, however, Eclectic Leaders recognize that the institutional goals of schooling—order, rules, control, and boundaries—are fundamentally opposed to the aspirational goals of school mission statements—freedom, disruption, autonomy, expression, and limitlessness.

Caught in the tug of war between the managerial realities of main offices and the educational ideals written into school mission statements, Eclectic Leaders orchestrate the right mix of managerial functions (implementation), leading functions (education), and championing functions (inventing) to make collective sense out of conflicting goals, values, and practices. There are no hard and fast organizational rules to govern the orchestration of the functions of Eclectic Leadership. The social and political environment of a leader's community will influence the functions that emerge out of the main office.

In mission-driven main offices, it is understood that none of the administrative roles assumed by Eclectic Leaders can stand alone: without new vocabularies and metaphors, teachers see no reason to adopt new learning theories and practices (championing role); without comprehensive training regimes, teachers lack the knowledge and skills to apply new learning theories and practices (leadership role); and without responsive organizational and instructional systems, teachers are blocked from fully enacting new learning theories and practices (managerial role).

No author on school reform can adequately describe those intangible leadership qualities that energize a school community to pursue new forms of teaching and learning: the courage to question the goals and values of institutional schooling; the imagination to create a new narrative for teaching and learning; and the practical wisdom to mediate the divide between theory and practice. All three leadership qualities weave together the why, what, and how of schooling into a narrative and plans of action that value the *ought* of classrooms over the *is* of main offices.

This entire book was aimed at providing school administrators with the managerial and leadership tools to live up to the educational ideals expressed in their school mission statements. What no book on educational reform can prescribe is the *will* to become an Eclectic Leader.

Only you can provide that.

References

Jones, A. C. (2015). *Becoming a Strong Instructional Leader: Saying No to Business as Usual*. New York: Teachers College Press.

Jones, A. (2018). *The First 100 Days in the Main Office: Transforming a School Culture*. Charlotte, NC: Information Age Publishing.

Sarason, S. B. (1997). *Revisiting "The Culture of the School and the Problem of Change"*. New York, NY: Teachers College Press.

Sergiovanni, T. J. (1992). *Moral Leadership: Getting to the Heart of School Improvement*. San Francisco: Jossey-Bass Pub.

About the Author

Dr. Alan C. Jones is an educational consultant specializing in curriculum, instruction, and instructional leadership. Dr. Jones was a middle school and high school teacher and served as principal of Community High School District 94 in West Chicago, Illinois for seventeen years. Under his leadership, Community High School was awarded the Blue-Ribbon School of Excellence and was recognized as a School of Excellence by HISPANIC magazine. His publications include numerous articles in educational journals on instructional leadership and school reform and four books: *Students! Do Not Push Your Teacher Down the Stairs on Friday: A Teacher's Notebook* (Quadrangle Books, 1972); *Becoming a Strong Instructional Leader: Saying NO to Business as Usual* (Teachers College Press, 2012); *Teaching Matters Most: A School Leader's Guide to Improving Classroom Instruction* Corwin Books, 2012); *The First 100 Days in the Main Office: Transforming a School Culture* (Information Age Press, 2018).